SCOTTISH BAKING

SCOTTISH
BAKING

SUE LAWRENCE

First published in 2014 by Birlinn Ltd

West Newington House

10 Newington Road

Edinburgh

EH9 1QS

www.birlinn.co.uk

Photography by Alex Hewitt

www.alexhewitt.co.uk

Design and layout by James Hutcheson and Tom Johnstone

ISBN: 978-1-78027-200-9

British Library Cataloguing in Publication Data
A catalogue record for this book is available from the British Library

Typeset in Adobe Garamond Pro at Birlinn

Printed and bound by Hussar Books, Poland

CONTENTS

DEDICATION

For Mum, with love

ACKNOWLEDGEMENTS

Thanks to Pat, Euan, Faith and Jess – for advising and eating.

And to Linda Dick, Sue Hadden, Margaret Horn, Claire Mckay, Isabelle Plews, Jess Plews, Alan Stuart and Jo Sutherland – for recipe ideas old and new, and for tasting!

Thanks as ever to Jenny Brown for her extraordinary patience and enthusiasm.

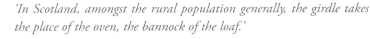

Introduction

'In Scotland, amongst the rural population generally, the girdle takes the place of the oven, the bannock of the loaf.'

F. Marian McNeill wrote this in her 1929 book *The Scots Kitchen*, and although it no longer rings true, since most kitchens nowadays have ovens, it perhaps explains the origin of some of our baking traditions. We have never had grand cakes or indeed many yeast-based breads or loaves, since the only way to bake bread with yeast (or brewer's barm as was often used) was to get a piece of bread-dough from the village baker, add some fruit and spices and ask the baker to bake it for you. Hey presto, the Selkirk bannock was born.

Our dependency on the girdle ('griddle' in countries other than Scotland) means that, to this day, we have a plethora of oatcakes and scones and pancakes baked upon the girdle. This is because the girdle, as well as the soup-pan, were probably the only pieces of equipment in a rural Scottish kitchen.

Nowadays, of course, we have many wonderful regional specialities that are not girdle based, and of course we have all our new-fangled imports, but in our nostalgic moments we still hark back to the old-fashioned bakes. There is a time and a place: sometimes only a tattie scone, warm from the girdle and dripping in butter, will do. At other times, a slice of indulgent millionaire's shortbread fits the bill just fine, thank you.

There is an old-fashioned little tea-shop along the road from me. Every time I pass, on the way to the bus stop, I have to stand still and sniff the air. For the smell coming through the door is so reminiscent of my childhood. It is sweet, sugary and buttery; it is shortbread being baked for tea, soda scones straight off the girdle,

border tart fresh from the oven. I can almost taste the crunchy sugar on top of the shortbread, the homely taste of the scone as the butter soaks into its warm soft dough and the buttery-sweet fruit mixture of the pastry-lined tart. There is no smell quite like it. In my opinion, you can forget the aroma of roasting coffee if you want to sell your house; get down and dirty with the flour and sugar and do some home-baking instead.

I have lived and breathed baking ever since I can remember. And in Scotland this does not mean fancy iced buns, cupcakes laden with piped icing or garishly decorated gateaux. No, for us in Scotland it is the homely smells of freshly baked scotch pancakes, treacle scones, jam and coconut tarts and of course shortbread – those things I smelled as I walked through the door after school that sum up Scottish baking. Nothing fancy – but oh so delicious.

The cake tins in my home – and everyone else's – were filled with baked goods such as sultana cake and fruit loaf for visitors popping in; it was all just part of growing up. And when my children were young, they too would come home to baking smells and to cookie jars filled to the gunwales.

The many church fêtes, school fairs and gala days of my youth featured home-baking stalls. And just like those today which are still allowed under the ludicrous health and safety legislation, the baking was and is always the first to go. There would be gingerbread, cherry and coconut slices, scones, home-baked biscuits and of course tablet wrapped in greaseproof paper, all laid out in serried rows, ready for the onslaught. The minute the doors opened, there was a rush, an unseemly surge towards the baking stall which was known to sell out in minutes. Heaven help anyone trying to reach the tombola stall if they were in the path of the baking fans, intent on their purchase.

Opposite: Dundee Cake and Dundee Cupcakes (p.51).

Scottish baking has evolved over the years, with old recipes adjusted to add less sugar and less of the unhealthier fats – but the traditional old favourites remain as popular as ever. Nowadays though, since baking has become the new hip pastime, there are many other baked goodies that we Scots love both to bake and devour. This book contains mainly traditional recipes, but also many new modern ones to tempt your tastebuds. There is always something – old or new – to satisfy our insatiable sweet tooth.

(** after the recipe name denotes contemporary recipes)

CHAPTER ONE

Bread and Bappery

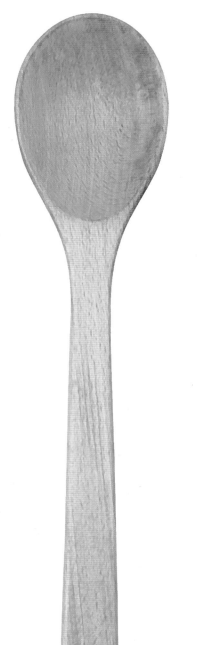

Bappery is a wonderful word coined by the actress Siobhan Redmond when she described to me what her aunts used to love making when she was growing up in Glasgow; to her it meant scones, cakes and teabreads, all the home-baking that we Scots were brought up on. But bappery is such an iconic term, I like to use it to describe all yeasted Scottish baking, whether it is for a butterie, a Selkirk bannock or of course a bap.

Over the centuries the type of breads that have been enjoyed in Scotland has varied enormously, from medieval trencher breads and sixteenth century wheaten loaves to the healthy twentieth century Doris Grant loaf and of course a myriad of regional oatmeal or barley meal bread in between. In most rural homes, however, there would have been no oven and so girdle breads and scones were more traditional.

The important thing to remember when baking any yeast-based recipe is that, since Scotland is an inherently cold country, you can often ignore some recipe instructions that say 'Leave to rise for an hour'. In Scotland, unless you live in a modern house with triple glazing and central heating on full blast, you need to give the dough plenty time to rise. My Victorian stone house has an airing cupboard which I sometimes use for bread dough to rise. Otherwise, it's my heated floor in the kitchen – but I place the bowl of dough on a wire rack, so it never has direct contact with heat. And even then it usually needs a couple of hours, not one hour, certainly in midwinter. Besides, in the olden days, it would have been a long slow process. And you know what? The bread would have tasted even better for that.

Opposite: Oatmeal Loaf (p.16).

I

BAPS

makes 12

Baps – or morning rolls as they are often called throughout Scotland – are perfect for breakfast as they are soft, floury and unchallenging as the first food of the day. It is only later on that you feel ready for a well-fired or crusty roll, which is not only noisy to eat, it can also be hard work on the jaws. In Aberdeenshire, morning rolls are called 'softies' if they have no flour on them and 'floury baps' if they do.

My parents both remember, from their Dundee childhoods, being sent to the baker's for morning rolls before breakfast on certain days – not every day, as porridge was the daily staple. Just as we have the vision of every French household sending someone for the morning baguette, so the Scottish family sent a minion (usually the youngest child) to the bakers for breakfast rolls.

According to F. Marian McNeill, in the sixteenth century baps were known as 'bawbee baps', a bawbee being the sixteenth and seventeenth-century term for a Scottish halfpenny.

Baps are wonderful split and spread with butter and eaten with bacon, egg, sausage or, my favourite, black pudding and tomato.

500g/1lb 2oz strong white flour, sifted	300–325ml/10–11fl oz milk and water (mixed), hand-hot (tepid)
1 heaped tsp salt	flour, to sprinkle
25g/1oz butter, diced	
1 x 7g packet of easy-bake dried yeast	

Mix the flour and salt in a bowl, rub in the butter, then stir through the yeast. Make a well in the centre. Gradually pour in enough of the tepid liquid to form a stiffish dough. Then, using lightly floured hands, bring together to form a dough. (I use a claw shape in both hands to draw together the dough.) Turn this out onto a lightly floured board and knead for about 10 minutes or until you can feel it change texture, from rough and nubbly to smooth and elastic. Place in a lightly oiled bowl and cover. Leave to rise somewhere vaguely warm for 1½–2 hours – or until well-risen.

Knock back the dough to punch out the air, then divide into twelve pieces. Shape each into a round by rolling lightly between the palms of both hands, then tuck any joins underneath, so that the top is convex. Place on a lightly oiled baking sheet and cover loosely. Leave for about 30 minutes – again in a vaguely warm place.

Then, using the heel of your hand, press down gently on each one to flatten slightly. Sprinkle lightly with flour. Bake at 220C/425F/Gas 7 for about 15 minutes, or until puffed up and golden brown. Eat warm.

2

SELKIRK BANNOCK

makes one large bannock

Reputedly a favourite teatime treat of Queen Victoria, this rich fruited sweet bread is a speciality of the Borders, having originated in the town of Selkirk as a means of using up spare bread dough. Selkirk bannock look-alikes are now made by bakers in other Border towns, such as Galashiels, Hawick and Kelso. Bakers nowadays do not, of course, make them as a means of using up a batch of basic dough by enriching with butter, sugar and sultanas, but it is interesting to read the basic guidelines for this method in F. Marian McNeill's The Scots Kitchen. *She writes:*

'Get two pounds of dough from the baker. Into this rub four ounces of butter and four ounces of lard until melted but not oiled. Then work in half a pound of sugar, three-quarters of a pound sultanas and a quarter pound of finely chopped orange peel. Put the dough into a buttered tin, let it stand for about thirty minutes to rise then bake in a good steady oven.'

Here is my more modern version (for those of us unable to buy two pounds of dough from the bakers!) for a magnificently bulging and moist bannock that is easy to make and all too easy to consume. Mine is a lot less sweet than most traditional ones, which have some 200g/7oz sugar, but I think the inherent sweetness of the dried fruit more than compensates. You can easily add an extra 25g/1oz sugar if you like. Also, since I am not keen on peel, I prefer to leave it out and use only sultanas. Besides, according to Theodora Fitzgibbon's Taste of Scotland, *it was originally only made with finest Turkish sultanas. Orange or mixed peel seems to be a rather more recent addition but I do like to add a hint of citrus by grating in some lemon zest. I am not sure Queen Victoria would have been amused by this frippery, though.*

1kg/2lb 4oz strong white flour	grated zest of 1 lemon, optional
175g/6oz butter, softened	approx. 500ml/18 fl oz milk and water (mixed), hand-hot (tepid)
2 x 7g sachets of easy-bake dried yeast	
70g/2½oz golden caster sugar	1 free-range egg yolk, beaten, to glaze
500g/1lb 2oz sultanas and raisins (or just sultanas)	

Sift the flour and a pinch of salt into a bowl, then rub in the butter till thoroughly combined. Stir in the yeast and sugar, then add the dried fruit and lemon zest.

Now add enough of the tepid liquid to combine to a soft but not sticky dough. Bring together with lightly floured hands then turn onto a floured board and knead well for 10 minutes or so until smooth. This is hard work with such a large mass of dough, but just think what it is doing for your upper arms!

Place in a lightly oiled bowl, cover and leave somewhere vaguely warm for about 2 hours, or until well-risen.

Shape into a bannock: a round flattened dome about 28cm/11in diameter. Place on a buttered baking sheet and brush all over with half the egg yolk. Leave for about an hour or until well-risen, then re-brush with yolk and bake at 220C/425F/Gas 7 for 10 minutes. Next cover loosely with foil to prevent any fruit poking out becoming burned, and reduce to 190C/375F/Gas 5 and continue to bake for about 30 minutes. It is ready once golden brown all over and when the base sounds hollow if tapped underneath. Leave to cool on a wire rack, then, once completely cold, slice and spread with butter.

3
BUTTERIES/ROWIES
makes 16

'I'm making do with a coffee and a rowie, the region's own flattened, salty version of a morning roll, designed to keep for a week on a heaving trawler or something, allegedly.' These words in Ian Banks' brilliant book Stonemouth describe Aberdeenshire's local bread beautifully.

And for those assuming something called 'butterie' must involve butter, sorry to disillusion you: it has never been traditional to use butter to make it. It was always 'white fat' or lard, although original Aberdeen fishermen's 'rowies' (Aberdonians refer to them as rowies; elsewhere they are butteries) were made with butcher's dripping or lard. They had been designed to last long, so the fishermen could eat them on long trips away at sea.

I prefer the flavour of butter, however. And though my recipe uses all butter, you could just as well make them with all lard for a truly authentic flavour. They are the perfect accompaniment to soup, salad or cheese. I don't think they need a thick smear of butter on top as is the norm in Aberdeenshire; to my taste they are buttery enough.

600g/1¼lb strong white flour	200g/7oz butter, softened
1 x 7g sachet easy-bake dried yeast	sea salt
1 level tsp golden caster sugar	

Make the bread dough by placing the flour in a bowl. Add the yeast, sugar and 2 tsp salt. Once well mixed, add enough hand-hot (tepid) water to combine to a dough: about 350ml/12 fl oz. Turn onto a board and knead for 7–8 minutes until smooth, place in large bowl, cover and leave somewhere vaguely warm for a couple of hours until risen.

Then punch down and roll out with your palms to form a rectangle. Cut the butter into three long slices. Add a third at a time to a third of the bread dough. Then fold over and continue with the remaining thirds. It is a folding process, like making puff pastry. Now, either knead by pushing and folding and turning the dough until you can see the butter is incorporated, or, if you prefer, using well-floured hands, 'chop' in the fat by hand, with the blade of a blunt knife, a pastry scraper or the long edge of a palette knife. Once well combined, the dough will be slightly sticky. (You will need to flour your hands throughout this preparation.)

Next cut into about 16 pieces and place these on a lightly floured (not buttered) large baking sheet. Shape them by pressing the front part of your (floured) hand – fingers only – once onto each, so they are flattened and dimpled with fingerprints. Sprinkle some sea salt over the top of each. Now cover with oiled clingfilm and leave to prove somewhere warm for another 30 minutes or so, then bake at 230C/450F/Gas 8 for about 20 minutes, until crispy and golden. Remove to a wire rack to cool.

4
HAGGIS FLATBREADS**
makes 6

The idea for these is inspired by those wonderful Middle Eastern flatbreads served with a spiced lamb topping. When you think about it, what is haggis but spiced lamb? So I thought I would give these flatbreads a try with Scotland's national dish – a Scottish cousin to what you will find all over the Middle East. They are delicious served as a snack or as a light supper with salad.

Flatbreads:	Topping:
500g/1lb 2oz strong white flour	tomato puree
1 x 7g sachet easy-bake dried yeast	about ¾ butcher's haggis
1 tbsp olive oil	olive oil
	large handful of mint and flat parsley, chopped

For the flatbreads, place the flour and yeast in a bowl and stir in 1 tsp salt. Make a well in the middle and pour in the oil, then 300–325ml/10–11fl oz hand-hot (tepid) water, enough to combine to a dough. Using floured hands, bring the dough together and knead on a lightly floured board for 8–10 minutes until smooth and elastic. Place in a lightly oiled bowl, cover and leave for 1–1½ hours somewhere vaguely warm until risen.

Punch down and divide into six. Roll out, with a rolling pin, to flat pitta bread shapes – elongated ovals. Place on two to three oiled baking sheets, loosely cover with oiled clingfilm and leave again somewhere vaguely warm for about half an hour, or until puffed up a little.

Next, smear about one teaspoon of tomato puree over each. Chop the haggis up and crumble over each bread, scattering it right out to the edges. Drizzle with olive oil and bake in a preheated oven (220C/425F/Gas 7) for about 20 minutes or until puffed up and golden.

Remove and scatter chopped mint and/or parsley over each one, drizzle with oil and serve at once.

5
BLACK BUN
serves 12–16

'There were stacks of Scots Bun, a dense black substance inimical to life, and full moons of shortbread adorned with peel or sugar plum in honour of the season and the family's affections.'

Robert Louis Stevenson, *Edinburgh Picturesque Notes.*

Though it is not one of my favourite dishes, I do not agree with Stevenson that black bun is 'inimical to life', though I can understand that the malevolent appearance of the black inners of its shiny golden pastry case might be off-putting to some black bun virgins.

In our house at Hogmanay there were some things that never changed. The home-made blackcurrant cordial might have been replaced by advocaat and lemonade as we became older, but there was always the tall dark man (my father) at the door at midnight with a piece of coal as the 'first-foot' of the year; and there was always black bun. Alongside the plate of shortbread with wedges of Cheddar cheese and sultana or cherry cake there was black bun – rich, heavy and dense – perfect to soak up the copious amounts of whisky proffered in every household. ('Just one more dram before you go…'). Black bun and 'shortie' were de rigueur everywhere, as we did the rounds of neighbours' houses, first-footing until the wee small hours.

Black bun was supposedly the original Twelfth Night cake eaten in Scotland, before it became known as 'Scotch Christmas Bun' during the first half of the nineteenth century: there is a recipe for a bun in Meg Dods' book of 1829. It was traditionally a spiced fruit mixture encased in a bread dough, but the bread dough gradually gave way to the lighter shortcrust pastry case and the name became simply black bun.

Although raisins, sultanas and currants are often interchangeable in recipes, here you must ensure the majority of the dried fruit is currants, for their black colour.

Pastry:

280 g/10oz plain flour, sifted

½ tsp baking powder

150 g/5½oz butter, diced

grated zest and juice of 1 lemon

beaten egg, to glaze

Filling:

450 g/1lb raisins

600 g/1¼lb currants

100 g/3½oz whole almonds, roughly chopped

50g /1¾oz walnuts, roughly chopped

150/5½oz plain flour, sifted

75g/2¾oz demerara or caster sugar

1 tsp ground allspice

1 tsp ground ginger

1 tsp ground cinnamon

½ tsp cream of tartar

½ tsp baking powder

2 tbsp whisky

approx. 4 tbsp milk

For the pastry, sift the flour and baking powder into a bowl, stir in the lemon zest. Rub in the butter, then add the lemon juice and 3–4 tbsp cold water, enough to bind to a stiff dough. Turn out onto a lightly floured board and roll out thinly. Use two-thirds of the pastry to line a buttered, square 23cm/9in cake tin. Roll out the remaining pastry to fit as a lid, cover and chill both the lid and the case for half an hour or so.

For the filling, mix everything together, except the whisky and milk. (I do this with my hands – it is easier.) Then add the whisky – and enough milk to moisten the mixture. Turn into the pastry case and press down well.

Dampen the edges of the pastry all round with a little water and place the rolled-out pastry lid on top. Press together the edges to seal, then cut off any remaining pastry. Prick all over with a fork. Using a very thin skewer, prick right through to the base of the tin: 6–8 pricks altogether. Brush the surface with beaten egg. (Retain a little egg.)

Bake at 140C/275F/Gas 1 for 2–2½ hours until golden-brown on top, reglazing with the remaining beaten egg after 1 hour of baking.

Cool in the tin for at least 2 hours, then carefully decant onto a wire rack to cool completely. Wrap in foil and store in an airtight container for at least 1 month – and for anything up to 3–4 months.

TRADITIONAL BLACK BUN
makes several buns

Here is a pre-war recipe from Walter Banfield, from his treatise on bread, which Master Baker Alan Stuart of Buckhaven sent me. I have not only kept the recipe as it was written nearly 100 years ago, I have also left the ingredients in imperial measures and Fahrenheit temperatures as I doubt many readers are going to use an entire sack of flour and twenty packets of dried fruit to make this at home. This is the bun that would have graced many a festive table in the big houses of Scotland over the centuries, until the pastry-encased bun which we now know and love gradually overtook this rather heavier version in popularity. I offer it to you here, however, more for the sake of nostalgia than for practical purposes.

Dough:	Fruit:
15lbs strong flour	10lbs seedless raisins
6 pints water	10lbs fleshy currants
3½ozs salt	3lbs orange peel
1oz yeast	1½lbs whole almonds

'The starting point is an overnight dough. Some of this is made into a short-paste by adding butter, whilst some is used slightly to aerate a very heavy mixture of fruits, nuts and spices. The fermented short-paste, which is extremely elastic, is used a casing for the filling in whatever tin is used.

Overnight keep dough at 72 degrees F.

After 12 hours, knock back and leave 1 hour before working off.

For casings work 2lbs butter into 9lbs dough.

Next work 14ozs butter and 6ozs mixed spices into 7lbs dough, then add the raisins, currants, orange peel and almonds.

A 2lb bun would need 2½ hours at 370 degrees F.'

7

OATMEAL LOAF

makes one loaf

This is an incredibly easy loaf to make. If you think you don't have time to knead by hand (or if you've just had your nails done) then fling the dough in a mixer with a dough hook for 5 minutes or so. It is delicious spread with butter and perhaps a slice of a tangy farmhouse cheese such as Orcadian Grimbister.

300g/10½oz unbleached strong white flour, sifted

150g/5½oz medium oatmeal

7g sachet of fast-action/ easy-blend dried yeast

Mix the flour, oatmeal and yeast in a bowl with 1½ tsp salt. Make a well in the centre and slowly pour in enough hand-hot (tepid) water (about 250–275ml/9–9½fl oz) to make a softish dough.

Using floured hands, bring the dough together and turn out onto a floured board, then, regularly sprinkling (lightly) with flour – I use a flour shaker – knead for 10 minutes until smooth. It should be soft and shiny-looking but not too sticky. Place in an oiled bowl and cover with clingfilm then leave somewhere vaguely warm for 1½–2 hours, until the volume is almost doubled.

Now punch down and divide into two, shaping into round loaves. Place on an oiled baking sheet and cover with oiled clingfilm. Leave to rise again, somewhere warm, for about 45 minutes or until, when the dough is gently pressed with your finger, it does not spring back.

Slash the top lightly with a knife to form diagonal slits across the middle, then dust lightly with flour and bake in a preheated oven (230C/450F/Gas 8) for 20–25 minutes or until the base sounds hollow when tapped.

8

PUGGY BUNS
makes 6

The recipe for this extremely old, traditional bun, the puggy bun, was kindly given to me some years ago by baker Kenny Adamson, whose Pittenweem bakery has its roots in the early seventeenth century. The bakery now specialises in producing some of the finest oatcakes in the country.

These individual-size buns look vaguely similar to an Eccles cake or Chorley cake. Puggies were made in Adamson's bakery for many years, certainly since Kenny's granny Agnes bought the bakery in 1887. The puggy buns, known locally as Hypocrites – white outside, black inside – are made these days with a shortcrust dough encasing a gingerbread-type mixture called gundy dough.

Gundy is the old Scots word for a spiced confection or sweetmeat. The gundy dough can be made up in advance and will last, in an air-tight container, for several weeks. The outer dough used to be a barm dough, then later a yeast dough: the puggy buns were the result of bakers using up leftover dough from their twice or thrice weekly batches of bread. Now a shortcrust pastry is used.

These Fife specialities are enjoyed as they are or spread with butter, and taste even better if first warmed under the grill.

Dough:

275g/9¾oz plain flour, sifted

125g/4½oz butter

Gundy:

175g/6oz strong flour, sifted

3 heaped tbsp golden syrup, warmed

50g/1¾oz golden caster sugar

1 heaped tsp bicarbonate of soda

1 heaped tsp mixed spice

50ml/2fl oz milk

Make the gundy first. Place the flour in a bowl, tip in the warmed syrup, sugar, soda, spice and milk and stir to combine. Bring together with a wooden spoon and wrap in clingfilm. Chill.

For the pastry, place the flour and butter in a food-processor with a pinch of salt. Process briefly until it resembles breadcrumbs, then add about 75ml/2½fl oz cold water (or enough to make a firm dough). Wrap in clingfilm and chill for an hour or so.

Roll out thinly. Cut out six circles, about 15cm/6in in diameter each. Divide the gundy into six and place a sixth of the gundy in the centre of each circle. Fold in the edges, then tuck them underneath and turn over. Roll out with a rolling pin to form a rough circle about 10cm/4in each.

Place on a greased baking tray and slit each three times on the top. Bake in a preheated oven (190C/375 F/Gas 5) for 20–25 minutes until a pale golden brown. Remove to a wire rack to cool.

9

BLACK PUDDING ROLLS
makes about 30 rolls

These rolls are like sausage rolls, but instead of sausage, you use black pudding. We are so lucky in Scotland to have many wonderful black puddings, which vary greatly in the use of fresh or dried blood and whether the onions are finely or coarsely chopped. Usually, however, Scottish black puddings have finely shredded suet, and this gives an overall appearance of, well, just plain black, unlike those Lancashire puddings and French boudins which are dotted with great unappetising-looking blobs of fat. In Scotland we know the fat is there, we just prefer not to look at it!

In Arthur Herman's book The Scottish Enlightenment, *there is a description of the Highlands in the early 1700s and the deprivation suffered by the typical Highlander, particularly in winter. 'Highlanders often had to bleed their cattle, mixing the blood with oatmeal and frying it in the fire. Sometimes cows were bled so frequently they could barely stand.'*

Nowadays, oatmeal is added to the blood in certain areas; many puddings are also made with barley. But most have a good nutty texture from oatmeal, barley or simply the onions. The best puddings have a clean aftertaste – and a definite urge to have more!

These rolls are ideal with drinks. Or, instead of cutting them into dainty little individual rolls, halve the long rolls and have for supper with perhaps a great dod of mustardy mash or a puree of peas and mint.

One of my favourites, Stornoway black pudding, is ideal for this recipe, not only in terms of shape, but also for its sublime flavour.

approx. 400g/14oz black pudding	milk
375g sheet of ready-rolled puff pastry	1 medium free-range egg, beaten
Dijon mustard	

Cut the puddings in half lengthways, then into long quarters.

Place the sheet of pastry onto a board. Spread three lines of mustard down the middle and lay the puddings on top: you will need to cut and shape a bit. What you are after is three long rolls.

Dab some milk round the edges of each bit of pastry and bring the pastry edges together. Cut along the edge so you have three rolls.

Now place the rolls, messy join-side underneath, on a baking tray lined with baking parchment. Brush the tops with beaten egg and chill well, retaining the remaining egg. (A double brush of egg ensures a wonderful golden crust with a truly glossy sheen.)

Remove from the fridge and re-brush with the remaining egg, then bake in a preheated oven (200C/400F/Gas 6) for 20–25 minutes or until golden brown and crispy.

Remove to a paper towel-lined board (to absorb any grease) and leave until cold before cutting into small pieces. Reheat before serving.

CHAPTER TWO

Scones

Scones form a substantial part of my childhood memories. Everyone's mums baked scones: they were no big deal, they were just always there, like mince or broth. Some were plain, some had currants or sultanas, some were mixed with syrup, some with buttermilk or sour milk to give an especially good rise. But they were just there, on the tea table, ready to be gently torn open with your fingers, then smeared with butter and jam; whipped or clotted cream was for effete southerners only.

And since they take only minutes to prepare and a mere 12 minutes to bake, scones are the perfect Fast Food – quick, easy and delicious! Split in half by pulling apart gently (never cut a freshly baked scone with a knife) then smear with butter and – unless it is a savoury scone – a good smear of jam. The whipped or clotted cream and jam ritual also has its place, but it is somehow not as homely as the butter-jam combo.

In Scotland, scones were traditionally 'baked' on the girdle in the days when only the big houses had ovens. Girdle scones (sometimes differentiated by being called soda scones) look different, are often triangular in shape and usually a little flatter than their oven-baked counterparts.

I

FRUIT SCONES
makes 8 large scones

There are many tips for producing the perfect scone but here are mine.

Handle the dough as little as possible and use the lightest touch you can. This is the time for happy thoughts – bad moods and table-bashing bread dough kneading will ensure a tough scone.

They must be eaten on the day they are made, barely warm, never hot.

The wetter the scone mix, the more successful your scones will be, but do not overdo the liquid or they will spread out sideways instead of rising elegantly upwards.

In Scotland a scone is a scone (pronounced like dawn), never a scoan and certainly never a skoon which is, however, how we pronounce the town outside Perth, Scone. Confused? Don't worry, just rustle up a batch of them; it will take you mere minutes to prepare, and only a few minutes more to bake.

You can substitute currants for the sultanas; and add some chocolate chips and a few crushed cardamom seeds for a change.

450g/1lb plain flour	75g/2¾oz sultanas
2 rounded tbsp baking powder	2 large free-range eggs
125g/4½oz butter, cubed	milk
40g/1½oz golden caster sugar	

Sift the flour and baking powder into a large bowl with a pinch of salt. Rub in the butter, then stir in the sugar and sultanas.

Lightly whisk the eggs in a measuring jug and add enough milk (approx 150ml/5fl oz) to make up to just under 300ml/10fl oz. Slowly add this to the bowl then very gently combine, first with a spoon or palette knife and next finally get in with floured hands to shape into a round. Place this on a floured board. Pat out gently to about 3cm/1¼in, then, using a large floured cutter, cut into 8 scones.

Place on a lightly buttered baking tray and brush with any leftover egg/milk in the jug (or add a splash more milk) then bake near the top of a preheated oven (220C/425F/Gas7) for about 12 minutes or until well-risen and golden on top. Leave to cool on a wire rack.

2

CHEESE SCONES
makes 8 large scones

My friend and colleague, Stephen Jardine, always says of a cheese scone: 'It's just plain wrong!' He simply doesn't get them. His assertion is that a scone should be served with butter and jam and is an inherently sweet thing. Even when I suggest serving a buttered cheese scone with soup in winter or a salad in summer, he winces. I could not disagree more about the merits of a freshly-baked cheese scone.

The variations on this basic recipe are endless. Add some finely chopped herbs (chives, thyme or oregano are good), a teaspoon of dried mustard or a few shakes of cayenne pepper to the mix. You can also cut the scones into tiny little rounds and serve them as canapés, split and topped with cream cheese or soft goats' cheese and then a sliver of smoked salmon, or roasted red pepper – or a halved cherry tomato . . .

They are infinitely versatile: and, when that amazing aroma of warm savoury scone permeates the whole house, how could they possibly be 'wrong'?

450g/1lb plain flour

2 rounded tbsp baking powder

125g/4½oz butter, cubed

250g/9oz grated mature Cheddar

cracked black pepper, optional

2 large free-range eggs

milk

Topping:

extra grated Cheddar

Sift the flour and baking powder into a large bowl then rub in the butter. Stir in the cheese and add a pinch of salt, and the pepper (if using).

Place the eggs in a measuring jug, stir lightly and add enough milk to make up to 300ml/10fl oz. (approx 150ml/5fl oz). Stir lightly, then add most of this to the mix (enough to combine to a softish dough), and gently combine, getting stuck in with your (floured) hands. Bring together gently (you do not need to knead, only bring the dough together) and place on a floured surface, patting out till about 3cm/1¼in high. Using a fluted cutter, cut out 10 large scones and place on a lightly buttered baking tray.

Brush the tops with any liquid left in the jug (add a splash more milk if necessary) and top with the extra cheese. Bake near the top of a preheated oven (220C/425F/Gas 7) for about 12 minutes or until golden and well-risen.

Remove to a wire rack and leave until barely warm, before splitting and spreading with butter.

3
TREACLE SCONES
makes 6

I have always loved treacle puddings and any baked goods involving black treacle. These treacle scones were part of my mother's regular home-baking repertoire when I was young; black treacle is hugely popular in Scotland, whether in steamed puddings, gingerbread or scones.

The other type of treacle scones I had as a child appeared at Halloween. Then we would attempt to bite thick, floury triangular scones that had been daubed in sticky black treacle. The snag was that they were hung by a string from the washing line in the kitchen (above a newspaper-covered floor, needless to say) and our hands were tied behind our backs. As a contrast to this the next game was always dooking for apples, which involved immersion of your face in tubs of freezing cold water for apples that always managed to bob away from you just as you were about to pounce. I always preferred the Halloween parties at houses with nice parents who would let you manoeuvre with a fork in your mouth to spear the apple instead of plunging your head into the tub itself. Admittedly this method did not help to clean the black sticky faces of treacle.

50g/1¾oz butter	½ tsp ground ginger
1 heaped tbsp black treacle	½ tsp mixed spice
225g/8oz self-raising flour	approx. 75ml/2½fl oz milk
¼ tsp baking powder	

In a small pan, heat the butter and treacle together over a low heat until just melted. Remove from the heat and allow to cool for about 5 minutes.

Sift the flour, baking powder, a pinch of salt and spices into a mixing bowl. Make a well in the centre, then pour in the treacle/butter mixture, with just enough milk to combine to a softish dough.

Lightly flour your hands and bring the dough together, using a very light touch with minimal handling (otherwise the scones will be tough). Pat out to a thickness of about 2.5cm/1in (with your hands – do not use a rolling pin). If there are any cracks, knead gently together to make smooth. Using fluted or round scone cutters, cut out six scones.

Place these on a buttered baking sheet and bake in a preheated oven (220C/425F/ Gas 7) for about 10 minutes until well-risen. Transfer to a wire rack to cool a little, before eating warm with butter.

4
POTATO SCONES
makes 8

Known more commonly as Tattie Scones, these are girdle scones often served for breakfast or tea. Sometimes I add about 25g/1oz grated Cheddar to the mixture and serve them with a bowl of broth or lentil soup for lunch. Eat them warm, with a thin smear of butter, whenever they are made; leftovers can be toasted the next day.

Use a floury potato such as Maris Piper, King Edward or Pentland Dell.

1 large potato (about 250g/9oz)	¼ tsp baking powder
25g/1oz butter	butter, to cook
50g/1¾oz plain flour	

Peel the potato, cut into chunks and cook in boiling water until tender, then drain well. Using a potato masher, mash the potato with the butter. Now weigh it: you need about 200g/7oz mash.

Sift the flour, ½ tsp salt and the baking powder into a bowl. While the mash is still warm, stir into the flour and combine well. Using lightly floured hands, gently shape this mixture into two balls and turn onto a lightly floured surface. With a rolling pin, roll out gently to form two circles about 5mm/¼in thick. Cut each circle into quarters. Prick all over with a fork.

Heat the girdle (or heavy frying pan) to medium-hot, smear over a little butter, then, once hot, transfer four scones to it with a large spatula or fish slice. Cook for about 3–4 minutes each side until golden brown. Transfer to a wire rack to cool briefly before spreading with a little butter and eating warm.

These can also be made in advance; loosely wrap in foil and reheat in a low oven.

5

SODA SCONES
makes 4–6

Traditionally baked on a girdle, they can also be baked in the oven (200C/400F/Gas 6 for 20–25 minutes). They are delicious split apart and smeared with butter and jam; or they are also wonderful with a hearty beef stew.

250g/9oz self-raising flour

½ tsp bicarbonate of soda

2 tsp golden caster sugar

1 medium free-range egg

25g/1oz butter, melted, cooled slightly

200ml/7fl oz buttermilk (or approx. 175ml/6fl oz milk)

First put on your girdle (or heavy frying pan) to heat to medium hot, smearing with a little oil.

Sift the flour and soda into a bowl with half a teaspoon of salt and the sugar. Make a well in the centre and add the egg, melted butter and enough buttermilk (or milk) to combine to a soft dough. Do not overwork.

Tip onto a floured board and, using floured hands (it is sticky) shape without kneading into a round about 22cm/8½in diameter. (It should be about 2cm/¾in thick). Using a floured knife, cut into quarters or sixths. Dust lightly with flour and transfer carefully to the hot girdle.

Cook for about 5 minutes (by which time they will have risen and have formed a fabulous brown crust underneath) then carefully flip each over. Continue to cook until done, on a lower heat. They are done when you press down lightly and there is no liquid oozing out of the sides; at this point the edges will be dry. It might take 15 minutes altogether, about 5 minutes for the first side and 8–10 minutes on the other. Transfer to a wire rack and serve warm.

6
MULL CHEDDAR MUFFINS**
makes 24 mini muffins or 16 regular-sized muffins

These are not, of course, scones, but they sit nicely beside cheese scones as they are more and more popular in cafes with a cup of tea or for brunch. Just as with scones, the trick is not to overmix; a light touch is all that's needed.

As well as good cheese, I like to add either leeks or ham – or, even better, both.

The regular-sized muffins are good with soup or salad for lunch; the mini muffins are ideal as canapés with drinks.

250g/9oz self-raising flour	1 tbsp finely snipped chives
125g/4½oz Mull Cheddar (or any other mature farmhouse Cheddar), grated – plus extra for topping	2 medium free-range eggs
	75g/2¾oz butter, melted and cooled a little
1 medium leek, trimmed, very finely sliced then chopped	2 tbsp natural yoghurt
	approx 100ml/3½fl oz milk
3–4 slices Parma ham, finely diced	

Sieve the flour into a bowl with a good pinch of salt. Stir in the cheese and then the leeks, ham and chives. Make a well in the centre and tip in the eggs, butter, yoghurt and enough milk to combine to a soft dough. Mix only briefly.

Fill 24 mini muffin cases or 16 regular-size muffin cases (not the huge American-size cases) and place on a baking tray. Scatter over some grated cheese.

Bake at 190C/375F/Gas 5 for about 20 minutes for the mini muffins and about 25 minutes for the regular ones, until risen and golden brown. Remove to a wire rack and leave until warm before devouring.

7
SOUR SKONS
makes 6–8

This is a modern variant on a traditional Orkney recipe. Classically the scone was made by soaking oatmeal in buttermilk for several days after which this – by now sour – mixture was mixed with flour and baking soda and baked on a girdle.

The flavouring of caraway seeds is traditional; the half teaspoon here gives only a suggestion of the aniseed flavour which I prefer. You can increase to 1 level teaspoon if you want to make the caraway flavour more prominent.

I like these served with a smear of butter and a sliver of cheese; goats' cheese works particularly well.

00g/7oz self-raising flour, sifted	½ tsp caraway seeds
25g/1oz medium oatmeal	142ml tub of soured cream
½ tsp baking powder	Approx. 2 tbsp milk

Place the flour, oatmeal and baking powder in a bowl and stir in the caraway seeds. Make a well in the middle and add the soured cream and enough milk to combine to a softish dough. Roll out gently to a thickness of about 2.5cm/1in, cut into scones and bake on a buttered baking sheet at 220C/425F/Gas7 for about 15 minutes or until well risen. Remove to a wire rack and eat warm, not hot.

8

OATMEAL SCONES

makes 6–8

*These are light, and with a good texture from the addition of the oatmeal.
Delicious with crusty clotted cream and home-made strawberry jam.*

150g/5½oz self-raising flour, sifted

75g/2¾oz medium oatmeal

½ tsp baking powder

75g/2¾oz butter, cubed

25g/1oz golden caster sugar

1 medium free-range egg

milk

Sift the flour, oatmeal and baking powder into a large bowl with a pinch of salt. Rub in the butter, then stir in the sugar.

Lightly whisk the egg in a measuring jug and add enough milk (approx 75ml/2½fl oz) to make up to 150ml/5fl oz. Slowly add this to the bowl (you might not need all the liquid – just enough to form a softish dough) and very gently combine with floured hands to shape into a round, then place on a floured board. Pat out gently to a thickness of about 2.5cm/1in and, using floured cutters, cut into 6–8 scones.

Place on a lightly buttered baking tray and brush with any leftover egg/milk in the jug (or add a splash more milk) and bake near the top of a preheated oven (220C/425F/ Gas 7) for 12–15 minutes or until well-risen and golden on top. Leave to cool on a wire rack.

9
CHEESE SAUCE SCONES**
makes 8–10

*These are like regular cheese scones, but with a divine topping of crusty
cheese sauce that is molten while warm. For the majority of Scots who love
anything to do with hot gooey cheese, these are the business! We are, after
all, the people who buy hot chips with grated cheese from the chippie and
burn our tongues as the cheese melts all over the chips.*

225g/8oz plain flour	milk
½ tsp baking powder	Topping:
75g/2¾oz butter, cubed	25g/1oz butter
125g/4½oz grated mature Cheddar	25g/1oz flour
	150ml/5fl oz milk
cracked black pepper	75g/2¾oz grated mature Cheddar
1 medium free-range egg	

First of all, make the thick sauce for the topping by melting the butter, adding the flour
and stirring constantly for a minute, then adding the milk and whisking until smooth –
about 3–4 minutes. Season with salt and pepper and stir in the cheese. Set aside to cool
while you make the scones.

Sift the flour and baking powder into a large bowl and rub in the butter. Stir in the
cheese, then add a pinch of salt and the pepper.

Place the egg in a measuring jug, stir and add enough milk to make up to 150ml/5fl
oz. Stir lightly again and add this to the mix, then gently combine, with floured hands.
Bring together gently (you do not have to knead, only bring the dough together) and place
on a floured surface. Pat the dough out till about 3cm/1¼in high. Using a fluted cutter,
cut out 8–10 scones and place on a lightly buttered baking tray.

Top each one with a level dessertspoonful of the sauce and bake in the middle of a
preheated oven (220C/425F/Gas 7) for 12–15 minutes or until golden and well-risen.

Remove to a wire rack and leave until barely warm before splitting and spreading
with butter.

CHAPTER THREE

Cakes

In Scotland, large cakes have traditionally been less common than girdle bannocks or scones. But as a treat, there are some classic Scottish cakes – Dundee cake, sultana cake and of course the different varieties of gingerbread.

Since, in Scotland, we never arrive at someone's house empty-handed, I think taking a cake as a present is even more thoughtful than taking the ubiquitous flowers, wine or box of chocolates. Rather than just nipping into the supermarket for a bunch of carnations, the gift of a home-made cake shows true care. And you will probably have some inkling of whether the recipient prefers an Orkney Broonie, moist and nutty with the oatmeal, to a dark and sticky gingerbread. Cakes evoke feelings of nostalgia, since as they bite into a sultana cake, the eaters recall perhaps a visit to their grandmother as a child. Or they remember a Dundee cake – dotted with those perfectly arranged almonds – bought after waiting in a long queue at the village fete during the halcyon days of childhood summers. But apart from the sentimentality aroused and the time and care you have taken over making your gift, there is also a fairly good chance that you will be offered some yourself! Traditional cakes vie for popularity with newcomers in this chapter; I like to think our cake-baking repertoire is enhanced by the more modern cake recipes. They are perhaps more show-offy than their classic counterparts but there's nothing wrong with a bit of un-Presbyterian flaunting on the cake walk!

Opposite: Sticky Apple Cake with Coconut Crunch (p.48).

I

GINGERBREAD
makes 1 loaf

The rich, dark cake we know nowadays as gingerbread has its origins as a hard ginger biscuit, flavoured with spices and dotted with dried fruit. Nowadays there are many regional gingerbreads throughout Scotland with a variety of ingredients, from Kirriemuir and Fochabers to Orkney.

Here is a basic recipe for a moist, treacly and delectably squidgy cake that is divine as it is or with each slice topped with a dod of butter.

200g/7oz butter	2 heaped tsps ground ginger
200g/7oz dark muscovado sugar	2 medium free-range eggs, beaten
225g/8oz black treacle (half a tin)	1 tsp bicarbonate of Soda
250g/9oz plain flour	75ml/2½fl oz milk, warmed

Heat the first three ingredients in a pan until liquid. Do not boil. Cool for a few minutes.

Meanwhile sift the flour, ginger and a pinch of salt into a big bowl and make a well in the centre. Add the eggs. Dissolve the bicarbonate of soda in the warm milk and add this to the 'well'. Slowly pour on the treacle mixture and mix everything well together. Tip into a buttered and lined 900g/2lb loaf tin.

Place in a preheated oven (180C/350F/Gas 4) for about 50 minutes, covering loosely with foil after 20 minutes or so. It is done when a wooden cocktail stick, pushed in, comes out almost clean; it can have a little moist crumb. Remove to a wire rack and leave until completely cold before cutting.

2

SULTANA CAKE

makes 1 cake

When I lick the bowl once I have put a sultana cake in the oven, the memory returns of being a little girl, standing on a kitchen stool and scraping every last vestige of cake batter from the bowl of Mum's sultana cake mixture. What did Proust know, with his dry old madeleines! Give me a moist, buttery sultana cake any day!

Mum's sultana cake – like her tea loaf, scones and pancakes – was available almost daily, ready to be decanted from the cake tins when people popped in, when it was tea time or simply when the only thing that would do was cake.

175 g/6oz butter, softened	175 g/6oz plain flour, sifted
175 g/6oz golden caster sugar	200 g /7oz sultanas
3 medium free-range eggs	1–2 tsp golden granulated sugar

Cream the butter and sugar well together – I do this in my food mixer, but you can beat by hand – until pale and creamy.

Beat in the eggs one at a time, with a third of the flour after each addition. Stir in a pinch of salt, add the sultanas and combine well.

Tip into a buttered, base-lined, deep 18cm/7in cake tin and bake at 170C/325F/Gas 3 for 1 hour, or until done (test with a cocktail stick: it should come out clean) switch off the oven and sprinkle the top of the cake with the granulated sugar. Return to the oven for about 3 minutes, then remove to a wire tray to cool.

STICKY APPLE CAKE WITH COCONUT CRUNCH**

makes 1 large cake

This squidgy apple cake has the most delectable crunchy coconut topping, and not only looks amazing, it tastes divine. My friend Isabelle's daughter Jess Plews told me about enjoying a piece of cake called a lumberjack cake in her local café, and I thought the ingredients would appeal greatly to our Scottish sweet tooth.

It is like sticky toffee pudding and Bounty bar (without the chocolate coating) rolled into one yummy cake. I defy you to stop at one slice.

175 g/6oz stoned dates, chopped	2 medium free-range eggs, beaten
1 level tsp bicarbonate of soda	*Coconut crunch topping:*
2 crisp green apples (such as Granny Smiths), peeled and chopped	75g/2¾oz butter
	150g/5½oz light muscovado sugar
100g/3½oz butter, diced	100ml/3½fl oz double cream
100g/3½oz golden caster sugar	1 tsp vanilla extract
75g/2¾oz light muscovado sugar	1 tbsp golden syrup
250 g/9oz self-raising flour, sifted	100g/3½oz shredded coconut (or half desiccated/ half coconut chips/flakes)

Place the dates in a large heavy saucepan with the bicarbonate of soda and 250ml/9fl oz boiling water. Warm over a low heat for 4–5 minutes until the dates are softened. Add the apples, then remove from the heat and stir in the butter. Once it has melted, add the sugars and flour. Once these are thoroughly – but gently – combined, stir in the eggs.

Pour into a buttered, base-lined, loose-bottomed 23cm/9in cake tin that is at least 10cm/4in deep. Bake on a foil-lined baking tray (in case of spillage) at 180C/350F/Gas 4 for 30 minutes.

Meanwhile, place the first five topping ingredients in another pan and bring slowly to the boil. Bubble away, stirring, for 2–3 minutes, then stir in the coconut and remove from the heat.

After the cake has baked for 30 minutes, remove and place on top of the cooker. Slowly spoon the coconut mixture all over the top; this has to be done gradually and gently so that the cake does not collapse under the sudden weight! Once this is done, place back in the oven and continue to bake for a further 30 minutes until cooked through, covering loosely with foil after 15 minutes or so. The cake bakes for about one hour altogether.

Remove, cool, then carefully transfer to a serving plate to serve.

4

MRS DOIG'S APPLE CAKE

makes 1 cake

I have adapted this delicious cake from one in Barbara Doig's recipe book, a fabulous personal collection of treats, from cakes and puddings to soups and sauces. My own favourite, meat-roll, is also in there. As a child, I used to love it when I was invited by Isabelle to stay at her house for tea, especially when her mum's meat-roll was being served.

Her apple cake recipe says it can be served warm for pudding or cold with a cup of tea.

175g/6oz self-raising flour	milk
½ tsp baking powder	*Topping:*
75g/2¾oz golden caster sugar	2 crisp eating apples
75g/2¾oz butter, diced	75g/2¾oz butter
finely grated zest of a lemon	150g/5½oz light muscovado sugar
2 medium free-range eggs	2 level tsp cinnamon
1 tsp vanilla extract	juice of half a lemon

For the cake, sift the flour and baking powder into a bowl with a good pinch of salt, stir in the sugar, then rub in the butter. Stir through the lemon zest.

In a measuring jug, crack in two eggs, add the vanilla and enough milk to make up to 150ml/5fl oz. Stir, then gently combine with the dry ingredients. Tip the batter into a buttered, base-lined deep 18cm/7in cake tin (with removable base) and smooth the top to level.

For the topping, thinly slice the unpeeled apples and arrange in closely overlapping rounds on the batter.

Melt the butter in a pan, add the remaining ingredients and, stirring well, bring to the boil. Stir for a couple of minutes, then spoon all over the apples.

Bake at 200C/400F/Gas 6 for about 30 minutes, covering loosely with foil for the last ten minutes to prevent the apples burning.

Remove and allow to cool before decanting.

5

DUNDEE CAKE AND DUNDEE CUPCAKES

makes one cake or 10 cupcakes

As a Dundonian, I am exceedingly proud of Dundee cake. Its origins are closely linked to the marmalade industry. The surplus of orange peel from the manufacture of Keiller's marmalade was used in Dundee cakes. A sign, therefore, of an authentic Dundee cake is the use of orange peel, not mixed peel. Unless you are a purist, however, mixed peel of good quality will still make a very fine cake.

The cake is a thing of great beauty, with its concentric circles of whole almonds on top. But I also love to make mini cakes, each in a muffin wrapper and each studded with an almond. These are ideal for picnics, preferably on a windswept Scottish beach.

175g/6oz butter, softened	150g/5½oz currants
175g/6oz golden caster sugar	150g/5½oz raisins
grated zest of 1 large orange	50g/1¾oz chopped mixed peel
3 medium free-range eggs	1 tbsp whisky (preferably malt)
175g/6oz self-raising flour, sifted	16–20 whole blanched almonds
½ tsp mixed spice	

Cream the butter, sugar and orange zest thoroughly until light and fluffy (I do this in my food mixer) then beat in the eggs one at a time, adding a teaspoon of the weighed flour with each egg to prevent curdling.

Sift in the flour, spice and a pinch of salt. Fold everything together gently, then stir in the dried fruits and mixed peel, together with the whisky.

For the cake, spoon the mixture into a buttered, lined 18cm/7in cake tin, levelling the top. Bake the cake in a preheated oven (150C/300F/Gas 2) for 1½ hours, then take it out and arrange the almonds on top in two circles. Return to the oven and continue to bake for a further 45 minutes (2¼ hours altogether).

Or spoon into 10 coffee shop-style muffin wrappers (or large muffin cases) set in a bun tin. Bake the cupcakes at 160C/325F/Gas 3 for about 35 minutes.

Once done (insert a wooden skewer into centre: there should be no raw batter on it), remove the cake or cupcakes to a wire rack to cool completely before decanting.

6

BROONIE

makes 1 loaf

The Orcadian broonie should not to be confused with Shetland's 'fatty brunnies', which are thick girdle scones or bannocks made of wholemeal flour or oatmeal. The Orkney broonie is a light, moist gingerbread not dissimilar to Yorkshire or Lancashire parkin. The names of both brunnie and broonie are from an Old Norse word – 'bruni' – which, according to F. Marian McNeill, means a thick bannock.

The broonie keeps well wrapped in foil, and is good either plain or buttered with a cup of tea. Alternatively, warm up thick slices and serve with a butterscotch sauce and a great dollop of clotted cream for a truly memorable pudding.

175g/6oz medium oatmeal	100g/3½oz light muscovado sugar
175g/6oz self-raising flour, sifted	1 medium free-range egg, beaten
2 rounded tbsp black treacle	150ml/5fl oz buttermilk (or fresh milk soured with ½ tsp lemon juice)
100g/3½oz butter, cubed	
2 tsp ground ginger	

Combine the oatmeal, flour and a pinch of salt.

Place the treacle in a small pan and heat very gently over a low heat until melted, then cool slightly.

Rub the butter into the oatmeal mixture, then stir in the ginger and sugar. Make a well in the middle and pour the treacle into the well, with the beaten egg and buttermilk.

Stir well until thoroughly combined, then pour into a buttered, base-lined 900g/2lb loaf tin.

Bake at 170C/325F/Gas3 for 50–60 minutes or until a skewer inserted into the middle comes out clean. Set the tin on wire rack and leave until cold before inverting.

7

PLUM CAKE
makes 1 large cake

This fabulous recipe is a combination of two very old Scottish ones, both beautifully written in a flowery hand. There is one recipe in an anonymous book from the late seventeenth century which has an elaborate recipe for a 'plume caike' starting 'Take 7 pounds of flower [sic] then take a pynt of creame and two pounds of butter . . .' It also has 22 eggs in it, so we are not talking small cakes! The other recipe is from Janet Maule's recipe book from 1701 and calls for 'a muchken of sweet cream' among other things. This second recipe I somehow feel an affinity with, as Janet lived in Panmure which is beside Dundee, my home town.

There is one ingredient in Janet Maule's recipe which is very interesting: she stipulates adding 'a pound of corduidron'. This is preserved quince, from a form of the old French word 'condoignac'. Though the English referred to it as 'chardquynce', Scots would have preferred the French to the English word (this is before the full Union in 1707, remember!). So I usually add some chopped quince paste (membrillo) to add even more flavour.

I have also found some early twentieth-century recipes for plum cake in Scotland that are similar, but often include black treacle which would make it richer and darker. Plum cake, just like plum pudding, was the term used to refer to any cake or pudding made with raisins or other dried fruits.

This cake, which has the same basic flavourings as the old recipes (some of which, from the 1700s, advocate adding 'some sweetmeats if you please'), is wonderfully moist. I imagine this probably comes from the unusual addition of cream.

Don't be put off by the inordinate number of ingredients! It is one of the nicest fruit cakes I know, and so easy to make.

400g/14oz self-raising flour, sifted

350g/12oz currants

50g/1¾oz raisins

50g/1¾oz mixed peel

grated zest of 1 lemon

grated zest of 1 small orange

75g/2¾oz quince paste, diced (optional)

½ tsp ground cinnamon

¼ tsp ground nutmeg

¼ tsp ground cloves

¼ tsp ground mace

250g/9oz butter, softened

150g/5½oz light muscovado sugar

3 large free-range eggs

100ml/3fl oz double cream

50ml/2fl oz medium sherry

Mix the first eleven ingredients together in a large bowl, with a pinch of salt. Beat the butter and sugar until thoroughly creamed and beat in the eggs one by one, then stir into the flour mixture with the cream and sherry.

Once well combined, spoon into a lined 22cm/8½in cake tin (ensure the paper is above the rim of the tin) and bake at 170C/325F/Gas 3 for 1 hour, then reduce to 150C/300F/Gas 2.

Place a piece of foil loosely over the top and continue to bake for a further 1¼ hours (2¼ hours altogether). Check it is cooked by inserting a skewer into the centre; it should come out clean.

Remove to a wire rack to cool before removing from the tin.

8
ORKNEY FUDGE CHEESECAKE**
serves 8

Any visitor to Orkney over the past couple of decades will be unable to leave the islands without trying what has become a local institution, the Orkney fudge cheesecake. Rich and creamy, it is made with the local fudge. Gorgeous.

It is easier to grate the fudge if it is well chilled first. Decorate with extra grated fudge or with seasonal berries.

250g/9oz Hobnobs (or other oaty biscuits), crushed

75g/2¾oz butter, melted

300g/10½oz Philadelphia cream cheese

300g/10½oz Orkney fudge, chilled

450ml/16fl oz double cream, lightly whipped

Make the base by combining the biscuits and butter and pressing into the base of a 24cm/9¼in springform cake tin that you have lightly buttered.

Beat the cream cheese until soft.

Grate the fudge (I use my food-processor) and tip most of it into the cream cheese, leaving some for garnish. Combine well then gently fold in the cream, combining slowly.

Spoon the cream mixture over the top and cover. Chill for at least 6 hours before scattering over the remaining fudge, carefully decanting and serving in wedges.

9

CLOUTIE DUMPLING

serves 12

'She tried some ham and a bit of the dumpling, sugared and fine, that Mistress Melon had made. And everybody praised it, as well they might, and cried for more helpings, and more cups of tea, and there were scones and pancakes and soda-cakes and cakes made with honey that everybody ate.' This description from Lewis Grassic Gibbon's Sunset Song, of the food at the novel's heroine Chris Guthrie's rural Aberdeenshire wedding in the early twentieth century, shows the crucial part cloutie dumplings played at special occasions.

In my Dundee family, it was made on birthdays instead of cake, and served on special occasions such as Christmas Day. My Auntie Muriel was the one, after my Granny Anderson died, to make a cloutie dumpling for members of the family on their birthdays. When I ask her for the recipe, she always says she couldn't possibly write it down, for she tells me there's a 'ticky of this and a ticky of that . . .': No-one ever wrote cloutie dumpling recipes down, they just made them. But I managed to pin her down and the following recipe is based on the one my family used to enjoy, with a few added extras, such as the black treacle to give it a rich dark flavour.

Cloot or clout is Scots for cloth, and so the name cloutie dumpling refers to the cloth in which the dumpling is boiled. Unlike any other dumplings or steamed puddings, it forms a characteristic 'skin', made by sprinkling flour and sugar into the cloth before filling with the mixture. Beware clouties without skin, as they are not authentic. The skin must be dried off before serving and this is done nowadays in the oven. As the youngest child, my mother's task was to dry off the dumpling in front of the open fireplace. She would sit there on a stool for 15–20 minutes, turning the dumpling round and round until it was dried off and ready to eat. Since it was made only for special occasions such as birthdays (in which case there were silver threepennies hidden inside, similar to charms in a Christmas pudding), this was a chore worth doing well. The dumpling would then be eaten with custard, but is now also served with cream or ice-cream. Next day, any leftovers would be served for breakfast, sliced and fried in rendered suet and eaten with bacon.

If you want to add them, wrap 5-pence pieces or charms in waxed or greaseproof paper and put into the mixture.

450/1lb self-raising flour, sifted

200 g/7oz golden caster sugar

½ tsp ground cinnamon

2 tsp mixed spice

150 g/5½oz shredded suet

450g/1lb mixed dried fruit (sultanas, currants, raisins)

½ tsp bicarbonate of soda

2 heaped tbsp black treacle

approx. 450ml/16fl oz full-cream milk (or single cream mixed with skimmed milk)

flour and caster sugar, to sprinkle

Mix the first seven ingredients together in a bowl with a pinch of salt, then drizzle over the treacle. Add enough milk to make a soft mixture of a stiff yet dropping consistency.

Dip a pudding cloth (or large tea-towel) into boiling water to scald, then drain well (I use rubber gloves to squeeze it dry) and lay out flat on a board. Sprinkle with flour and then sugar (I use my flour and sugar shakers): you want an even – but not thick – sprinkling. (This forms the characteristic skin.)

Now spoon the mixture into the middle of the cloth in a heap, then draw together the corners of the cloth and tie up securely with string, allowing a little room for expansion. Place the cloutie on a heatproof plate in the bottom of a large saucepan. Top up with boiling water to just about cover the pudding (it must come at least three-quarters of the way up the side), cover with a lid and simmer gently for about 3¾–4 hours, until it feels firm. Check the water level regularly and top up if necessary. You should continually hear the reassuring, gentle shuddering sound of the plate on the bottom of the pan for the entire duration of cooking.)

Wearing rubber gloves, remove the pudding from the pan and dip briefly into a bowl of cold water (no more than 10 seconds) so the skin does not stick to the cloth. Cut the string, untie the cloth and invert the dumpling onto a warmed ovenproof plate.

Place in the oven (180C/350F/Gas 4) for 10–15 minutes to dry off the skin – it should feel a little less sticky – then sprinkle with caster sugar and serve hot with custard.

CHAPTER FOUR

Traybakes and Teabreads

Although the word traybake is known everywhere these days, a more Scottish terminology is teabread, which is less used but simply encompasses, in many parts of Scotland, all manner of home baking to accompany a cup of tea. In Aberdeenshire, a 'fly cup' (of tea) is invariably accompanied by a 'fine piece', which means something extremely tasty, usually sweet, and always home-baked.

Traybakes are now hugely popular, whether to be sold at school fairs or packed neatly into lunch boxes or picnic hampers; they are exceedingly tasty and deeply satisfying. And although my childhood was filled with such delicious treats as peppermint crumble bars, chocolate cherry and coconut slice and paradise slice, nowadays we have a plethora of new and exciting traybakes to add to these traditional favourites.

These are ideal to have lurking in the kitchen in a cookie jar, ready to have with a cup of tea or morning coffee. Not as impressive-looking as a whole cake but just as welcome.

Opposite: Chocolate, Coconut and Cherry Traybake (p.67).

I

PARADISE SLICE

makes about 20 slices

This is another childhood favourite – pastry, jam and a fruit-studded coconut cake mixture on top. Paradise!

250g/9oz golden caster sugar	100g/3½oz undyed glacé cherries, halved
75g/2¾oz ground almonds	approx. 6 tbsp home-made raspberry jam
75g 2¾oz desiccated coconut	*Pastry:*
200g/7oz butter, softened	250g/9oz plain flour, sifted
2 large free-range eggs	50g/1¾oz ground almonds
150g/5½oz rice flour (also called ground rice)	25g/1oz golden caster sugar
	150g/5½oz butter, diced
250g/9oz sultanas	1 large free-range egg

For the pastry, place the flour, almonds and sugar in a food-processor, combine briefly, then add the butter and whizz until it resembles breadcrumbs. Now slowly add the egg through the feeder tube, stopping the machine the minute it starts to form clumps. Clingwrap and chill for half hour or so, then roll out to fit a lightly buttered Swiss-roll tin (23 x 33cm/9 x 13in). Prick all over and chill well, preferably overnight.

Next, bake in a pre-heated oven (200C/400F/Gas 6) for 10–15 minutes until just cooked but before the edges brown. Remove and cool briefly, then spread with the jam. Lower the oven to 180C/350F/Gas 4.

Place the sugar, almonds and coconut in a food-processor, whizz briefly and add the butter. Process until combined, add the eggs and rice flour, process briefly again, remove from the processor to a bowl and stir in the dried fruit. Spoon this carefully over the jam, smoothing the surface.

Bake for about 40–45 minutes or until golden-brown and set, covering loosely with foil after half an hour if browning too quickly. Remove to a wire rack, cool and cut into slices.

2
COCONUT FUDGE SQUARES**
makes 24–30

This divine recipe is adapted from Anta Pottery's 'Magic Bars' which I discovered at Anta's Café near Tain in Ross-shire.

The taste is coconutty, fudgy, chocolatey and biscuity. What's not to like?

150g/5½oz butter, melted

400g/14oz digestive biscuits, crumbed

405g tin of condensed milk (light condensed milk is fine)

250g/9oz quality milk chocolate, chopped into tiny chunks

175g/6oz desiccated coconut

Mix the butter and biscuits together and spread into a lightly buttered Swiss-roll tin (23 x 33cm/9 x 13in), pressing down firmly to level.

Slowly pour over the tin of condensed milk, leaving a tiny margin around the edges so it does not stick to the sides.

Scatter over the chocolate, evenly distributing it.

Finally top with the coconut and pat down firmly with the palms of your hands to ensure it is compact.

Bake in a preheated oven (180C/350F/Gas 4) for about 20 minutes until golden brown, covering loosely with foil after 15 minutes if the coconut is becoming too brown. Cool before cutting into bars.

3
GINGER OATY SLICE **
makes 24–30

My New Zealand friend Claire Mackay has a wonderful local café near her home in Wellington which serves the best ginger slice in the land. Andrea Holmes, who runs the Wadestown Kitchen in Wellington, has converted a basic flapjack recipe into this divinely rich ginger concoction.

The heavy use of oats in it is enough to bring it into the pantheon of Scottish-inspired bakes, and also, since Anthea is from Dunedin, the town named after the Gaelic name for Edinburgh, Dun Eideann, it more than merits inclusion here.

250g/9oz butter	*Topping:*
150g/5½oz light muscovado sugar	250g/9oz butter
	450g/1lb icing sugar
6 tbsp golden syrup	6 tbsp golden syrup
400g/14oz porridge oats	4 tsp ground ginger
100g/3½oz plain flour	a few chunks of crystallised ginger, diced
2 tsp ground ginger	

For the base, melt the butter, sugar and syrup together, then add the oats, flour and ginger. Mix well, and tip into a baking parchment-lined Swiss-roll tin (23 x 33cm/9in x 13in), press down to flatten and bake in a preheated oven (190C/375F/Gas 5) for about 20 minutes until golden. Remove to a wire rack to cool.

For the topping, combine everything except the crystallised ginger in a large saucepan, stirring over a gentle heat until the butter is melted. Stir constantly until you have a smooth glossy paste, then add in the crystallised ginger. Pour this over the cooled base and leave to set before cutting.

4
OATY BRAMBLE SQUARES**

Makes 18–20

All over Scotland, the berries known as blackberries in England are called brambles, whether they are wild or cultivated. Wild brambles of course have a much more intense flavour but the whopping farmed ones are far easier to come by; although there are few foraging trips more satisfying than going brambling. Just be sure you don't tell anyone else where you found the bushes, or next year the berries could all be gone by the time you set off with your basket.

These moist little treats are great for picnics or to enjoy with an afternoon cuppa. Don't use frozen brambles, as they will be too soggy and dampen the light, coconutty sponge.

200g /7oz self-raising flour

100g/3½oz porridge oats

200g/7oz butter, diced

250g/9oz light muscovado sugar

75g/2¾oz desiccated coconut

3 medium free-range eggs, beaten

350g/12oz fresh brambles (blackberries)

Place the flour, oats and a pinch of salt in a bowl and rub in the butter, until it resembles breadcrumbs. Stir in the sugar and coconut, then remove about 4 heaped tablespoons of the mixture and set aside. To the main bowl, slowly add the eggs, stirring until combined, and tip this into a baking parchment-lined 23cm/9in baking tin. Press down with the back of a spoon and scatter over the brambles. Spoon over the remaining mixture and press down gently with the palms of both hands.

Bake at 180C/350F/Gas 4 for 55–60 minutes or until golden brown and cooked through. Remove to a wire rack and cool before cutting into squares.

5
COFFEE BUNS
makes 12

Not dissimilar to rock buns, coffee buns were always part of the cornucopia of Scottish home baking. Some recipes use soft brown sugar but the ones below have a texture almost like a softer giant American cookie, though not as crisp. Most old recipes use margarine, but I always prefer the flavour of butter. Milk can be used instead of egg to glaze, though egg is traditional, as it makes the top glossier.

150g/5½oz butter, softened

150g/5½oz unrefined demerara sugar

1 large free-range egg

1-2 tbsp coffee essence (or strong black coffee, cooled)

300g/10½oz self-raising flour, sifted

50g/1¾oz currants

beaten free-range egg yolk, to glaze

Cream the butter and sugar together then beat in the egg then the coffee essence. Add the flour and a pinch of salt then, using your hands, roll into 12 balls. (Add an extra tablespoon of coffee if the mixture is too bitty; the dough should come together easily in your hands.) Place on a greased baking sheet and flatten slightly.

Brush the top with egg then bake at 190C/375F/Gas 5 for about 15 minutes or until golden and just firm. Remove to a wire rack to cool.

6

CHOCOLATE, COCONUT AND CHERRY TRAYBAKE**

makes 28 squares

This was part of my childhood. Though my mum did not make it, I used to enjoy it – in fact, adore it – at various friends' houses, and I have always loved it. It is a doddle to make, but you must leave the tray in the refrigerator for the specified time so the chocolate can fully set after it has been baked. If you try to lever out the pieces while the chocolate is still soft, it will simply all collapse on you.

450g/1lb quality chocolate (I like two thirds milk, one third dark)

200g/7oz natural (uncoloured) glacé cherries

4 medium free-range eggs

175g/6oz golden caster sugar

250g/9oz desiccated coconut

Melt the chocolate over a double boiler (or in a microwave on medium), then pour into the base of the prepared tin (a buttered Swiss-roll tin – 23 x 33cm/9 x 13in).

Smooth out with the back of a spoon. Allow to cool and harden.

Halve the cherries and place at intervals over the chocolate.

Beat the eggs in a bowl and add the coconut and sugar. Stir until well combined, then carefully spoon this mixture over the cherries, taking care not to push the cherries into one corner. Pat down gently to smooth the surface.

Preheat the oven to 350F/180C/Gas 4. Bake for about 25 minutes until the coconut mixture looks golden brown and feels firm to the touch.

Leave to cool for at least 30 minutes before marking into squares, then allow to become cold. Place in the refrigerator for at least 30 minutes until completely hard and cold, then remove the squares from the tin.

7

FLAPJACKS WITH BITS AND PIECES**

makes 18–24

Flapjacks are not traditionally Scottish, but they seem to sit very nicely here, given their oatiness!

These ones are bulging with all sorts of goodies – I have suggested certain seeds, nuts and fruit but you can substitute many other types. Chopped dried apricots, chopped almonds, dried blueberries or cranberries are all good.

You can omit the flour and use all oats (in which case use 400g/14oz oats); this gives a slightly chewier texture and is less easy to cut into neat slices, but is perfect for those who prefer to avoid wheat flour.

175g/6oz butter	50g/1¾oz raisins, dried blueberries or dried apricots
3 tbsp golden syrup	
150g/5½oz light muscovado sugar	50g/1¾oz desiccated coconut or toasted chopped almonds
350g/12oz porridge oats	
50g/1¾oz plain flour	25g/1oz sunflower seeds
½ tsp bicarbonate of soda	25g/1oz pumpkin seeds

Melt the first three ingredients together, then stir in the oats, flour and a pinch of salt. Stir in the remaining ingredients and tip into a lightly buttered Swiss-roll tin (23 x 33cm/9 x 13in), spreading out to level the surface.

Place on a large baking tin (in case of spillage) and place on the middle shelf of a preheated oven (180C/350F/Gas 4) until golden brown but still slightly soft – about 18–20 minutes – then remove to a wire rack. Cut into bars while hot, but only remove from the tin once cold.

8
OATY TOFFEE CRUMBLES**
makes 24

These are decadent in the extreme and yet, with the addition of oats, not entirely unhealthy! I usually use regular plain toffee for this, but treacle toffee makes a nice change.

125g/4½oz porridge oats	150g/5½oz butter, diced
200g/7oz plain flour, sifted	150ml/5fl oz full-cream milk
150g/5½oz light muscovado sugar	200g/7oz plain toffees
½ tsp bicarbonate of soda	

Place the oats, flour, sugar and bicarbonate of soda in a food-processor with a pinch of salt. Process briefly, then add the butter and process briefly again until the mixture starts to stick together.

Press about three-quarters of the mixture into a buttered Swiss-roll tin (23 x 33cm/9 x 13in), spreading out with (floured) hands to form an even base.

Place the milk and toffees together in a saucepan and heat over a low heat, stirring, until melted and smooth: this takes about 10 minutes.

Pour this slowly over the base and sprinkle the remaining oat mixture over the top, like a crumble topping. Bake in a preheated oven (180C/350F/Gas 4) for about 20 minutes or until the edges are golden brown. Cut around the edges to loosen, then leave on a wire rack to cool completely before cutting into small squares.

CHAPTER FIVE

Shortbread

In her book on the Scots household in the eighteenth century, Marion Lochhead writes about tea-parties of the day, when the hostess 'must have a plate of bun and one of shortbread – either in a cake, broken into bits, or in little, round nickety Tantallon cakes, or in the favourite "petticoat tails" . . .'

Many years on, it still appears at all the best tea-parties and also on special occasions such as Hogmanay (sitting alongside the black bun) but is still as regular a feature in Scottish kitchens as porridge or mince.

As for the ingredients: only the best will do. Never substitute margarine for the butter, since the whole point of shortbread is its buttery taste. A dough of all plain flour makes good shortbread but you can vary this by incorporating some rice flour (for a good crunchy texture), cornflour for a melt-in-the-mouth feel or farola (fine semolina) for a texture between the two.

Remember that shortbread should never be kneaded for longer than it takes to bring the dough together quickly in your hands. Overworking it will toughen the shortbread. Indeed I seldom roll with a rolling pin, I just press out lightly to the required shape before baking. The lightest hand possible will give the lightest shortbread.

I
PETTICOAT TAILS

makes 16 triangles

Shortbread has been made over the centuries in finger-shaped biscuits, round biscuits and a full round 'cake' known as petticoat tails. The origin of the name of these dainty shortbread biscuits is interesting. Some believe it to be a corruption of the French 'petites galettes' which is taken to mean little cakes. Given the Auld Alliance and the culinary interchange between France and Scotland, this is a possibility. Perhaps however it was even more simple. It is more likely in fact to do with the shape of the biscuits: the wedges are identical in shape to the individual gores of the full, bell-hooped petticoats worn by the ladies at Court – certainly at the time of Mary Queen of Scots in the sixteenth century, who was said to be fond of them.

A trick to ensure perfectly even petticoat tails is not to roll out the dough to completely fill the tin but to allow it to be just a little shy of the edges. That way the dough expands during baking to fill the tin and cooks evenly.

Traditionally there would be a round circle in the middle of the triangles but this is seldom seen nowadays. I like to use fine semolina or rice flour, but if you prefer a more melting texture, use cornflour.

175g/6oz butter, softened	75g/2¾oz cornflour, sifted or fine semolina or rice flour
75g/2¾oz golden caster sugar + extra to sprinkle	
175g/6oz plain flour, sifted	

Beat the butter and sugar together until really creamy and pale: this will take 4–5 minutes in a food-mixer or longer by hand.

Now add the combined flour, a good pinch of salt, and the cornflour/semolina/rice flour, a tablespoonful at a time, only adding more when each is incorporated. When it is all mixed in, bring together with your hands and divide into one large or two medium balls.

Roll out each ball (either by pressing with your palms if you have cold hands or with a very light touch of a rolling pin if your hands are hot) to a circle just a little shy of the size of your prepared tins (one lightly buttered 25cm/10in or two 17cm/6½in sandwich tins) then pop into the tin. Prick all over with a fork (ensure you go right through to the base) and 'scallop' the edges by nicking round the edges with the edge of a spoon. If you have time, chill the tins for about 10 minutes as the dough will be slightly warm, depending how hot your hands are.

Place in a preheated oven (150C/300F/Gas 2) for 35–40 minutes for the small tins and 40–50 minutes for the large tin, until a pale golden brown. Remove the tins to a wire rack, cut each into eight triangles and sprinkle over some sugar. Leave for 15–20 minutes or so, then remove from the tin while still a little warm but firm enough to be removed. Leave on a wire rack until cold.

2

SHORTBREAD

makes 24–30 little shortbread biscuits

This recipe is fail-safe and incredibly easy. I make it in my food mixer, but you can do it easily by hand. 'Softened butter' means soft enough that, when you press your finger into a block, there will be an indent; do not make it too soft or it will melt.

I like to use caster sugar and plain flour, but Jo Sutherland at Carfraemill Hotel in the Borders uses icing sugar and self-raising flour for her fabulous shortbread. Her Granny Joanna MacEwan from Caithness, who continued to bake well into her late 80s, made it this way. Jo rolls her dough out thinly, then cuts into little round shortbread biscuits; if you do this, they will take only 25 minutes to bake.

I prefer the ease of tipping everything into a baking tin, then cutting into bars or squares.

The icing sugar and self-raising flour combo give a very light, melting texture; the caster sugar and plain flour give more of a light crunch. Both are delicious.

280g/10oz butter, softened

140g/5oz golden caster sugar or icing sugar, sifted

280g/10oz plain flour (or self-raising), sifted

140g/5oz cornflour, sifted

golden caster sugar, to dredge

Place the butter and sugar in a mixer or food-processor and cream until pale. Once well amalgamated, add the flour, a good pinch of salt and cornflour a tablespoon at a time, and continue to blend briefly, just until thoroughly combined. Tip into a buttered Swiss-roll tin (23 x 33cm/9 x 13in) and, using floured hands, press down so it is level all over. Prick all over and now, if you have time, chill for 10 minutes or so.

Bake at 150C/300F/Gas 2 for 45–55 minutes. What you are looking for is a uniform pale golden all over. Do not allow it to become golden brown.

Remove from the oven and dredge all over with caster sugar, then cut into squares or bars. Leave for 10 minutes or so before carefully decanting onto a wire rack to cool.

3

CHEESY SHORTIE**

makes about 30 biscuits

Shortbread is often referred to as shortie in Scotland, and these little two-bite biscuits, though untraditional, are a wonderful addition to the lexicon of shortbread recipes, with their light crisp texture and mustardy, cheesy flavour. They are ideal to serve as canapés with drinks.

150g/5½oz plain flour, sifted

100g/3½oz finely grated parmesan cheese

¼ tsp cayenne pepper

100g/3½oz chilled butter, cubed

2 large free-range egg yolks

1 tsp Dijon mustard

Place the flour, cheese, cayenne and half a teaspoon of salt in a food-processor. Add the butter and whizz until it resembles breadcrumbs.

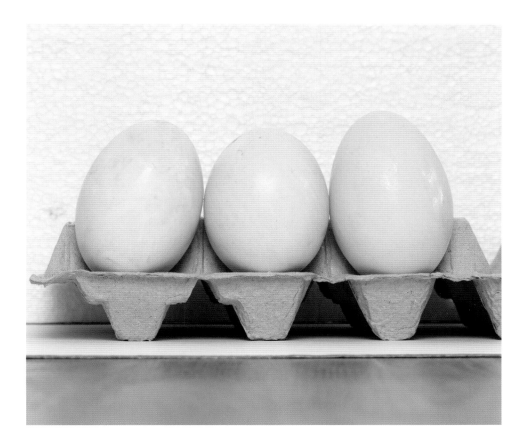

Mix the yolks and mustard, then add this with the motor running, whizzing briefly until combined.

Tip onto a large sheet of clingfilm and shape into a long roll, about 25cm/10in long. Pretend you are rolling out a long sausage with plasticene. Now either chill for a couple of hours or – even quicker – freeze for about 15 minutes until firm but not yet frozen.

Cut into thin discs, about the thickness of a pound coin, and place on a lined baking sheet. Prick lightly with a fork, then bake at 160C/325F/Gas 3 for 25–30 minutes or until a pale golden-brown. Remove carefully to a wire rack; they will still be a little soft, but will crisp up on cooling.

4
MILLIONAIRE'S SHORTBREAD**

makes about 24 slices

There are so many variations of this divine treat: for example instead of making a shortbread base from scratch, combine shortbread biscuits (about 300g/10½oz) with about 50g/1¾oz melted butter and press into the base of the tin.

Or you can add whole roasted hazelnuts – scatter these over the caramel before topping with chocolate.

Or you can use a chocolate ganache (chocolate and cream mixture) instead of melted chocolate for the topping.

I like to add some sea salt flakes for a contrast of flavour, the saltiness a great foil to the sweet filling.

You can also decorate the chocolate topping, once hard, by melting a couple of handfuls of toffees in a little milk until runny, then drizzling over the set chocolate.

Shortbread base:	Filling and topping:
225g/8oz butter, softened	2 x 397g tins of caramel or 2 x 397g tins condensed milk
100g/3½oz golden caster sugar	
225g/8oz plain flour, sifted	1 heaped tsp sea salt flakes, optional
100g/3½oz cornflour, sifted	300g/10½oz quality chocolate (I like one-third milk, two-thirds dark)

If you are using tins of condensed milk for the filling, you need to start the day before: place the unopened cans on their sides in a heavy saucepan and cover with boiling water; the water should almost cover the tins. Cover and simmer for 2 hours, checking the water and topping up with boiling water if necessary. Remove the cans and cool completely before opening.

For the base, cream the butter and sugar together well, until pale. (I do this in a food mixer; you can do it by hand if you prefer.) Now add the flours, a pinch of salt and blend briefly, until combined. Tip into a prepared tin (a Swiss-roll tin, 23 x 33cm/9 x 13in), lined with baking parchment: the best way to do this is to use two long strips, one going across, one down). Using floured hands, press down to make it level all over, then prick over gently with a fork. Bake in a preheated oven (150C/300F/Gas 2) for about 40 minutes or until a uniform pale golden all over. Remove and cool.

For the filling, spoon the caramel over the shortbread base. If using, sprinkle over the sea salt. Melt the chocolate and pour over the top, tipping the tin from side to side to spread the chocolate evenly over the surface. Place in the fridge to set, but remove and mark into squares after about 20 minutes (or before the chocolate becomes completely hard).

Once completely set (2–3 hours later), remove from the tin onto a board, using the two pieces of baking parchment to lift it. Using a hot sharp knife cut all the way through the base and, taking it slowly, cut all the pieces, running the knife under a hot tap and wiping dry before each slice.

Try not to eat too many slices in one sitting.

5

DATE CRUMBLE SHORTBREAD**

makes 16–20 squares

These little squares are delicious with a cup of tea – or perfect to take on picnics. Be sure to leave them till completely cold in the tin or they will collapse. Patience!

	Shortbread:
200g/7oz dried dates, stoned and chopped	200g/7oz butter, slightly softened
25g/1oz butter	100g/3½oz golden caster sugar
grated zest of 1 orange	
3 tbsp orange juice	250g/9oz plain flour, sifted
1 tbsp (2 balls) stem ginger	50g/1¾oz semolina
2 tbsp syrup from stem-ginger jar	1 tsp demerara sugar

Place the first six ingredients in a pan and bring to the boil, then lower the heat and simmer, covered, for about 5 minutes or until the dates are soft. Remove from the heat, tip into a small food-processor and whizz. Allow to cool.

For the shortbread, beat the butter and caster sugar together until light and fluffy – about 10 minutes – then gradually add the flour and semolina and a pinch of salt. Combine very briefly, until it just comes together as a dough.

Tip two-thirds of this mixture into a buttered, square, 23cm/9in tin, pressing down, then top with the cooled date mixture, spreading it out. Break the remaining shortbread into nuggets and dot all over the dates. Press down lightly with the palms of your hands and bake in a preheated oven (170C/325F/Gas 3) for 30–40 minutes until golden. Remove to a wire rack and sprinkle with the demerara sugar.

Cut into squares while hot, then leave until cold before removing from the tin.

6

PITCAITHLY BANNOCK
makes about 24

I have adapted this recipe from one found in a handwritten recipe book I was privileged to look at in the National Library of Scotland. The book was written by a Margaret Stewart in 1799. She lived in the Manse in Erskine, near Glasgow, where her husband was minister.

The addition of caraway seeds, nuts and peel was very commonplace in those days. For us it is so easy to buy almonds already blanched, but we tend to forget that before starting to make this in the old days, the cook would have had to blanch the almonds before chopping.

Before baking, the Pitcaithly bannock was often decorated: F. Marian McNeill writes in her recipe, 'Ornament, if desired, with large caraways and orange peel.'

The Pitcaithly bannock was a festive shortbread made for special occasions and was traditionally baked in a round, rather like a round of petticoat tails; so you can make my recipe here in two small sandwich tins, 18cm/7in each, following the instructions for the final stage of my petticoat tails.

225g/8oz butter, slightly softened

100g/3½oz golden caster sugar + extra

200g/7oz plain flour, sifted

100g/3½oz rice flour (ground rice)

1 heaped tsp caraway seeds

40g/1½oz finely chopped almonds

grated zest of 1 small orange

Place the butter in a food mixer with the sugar. Cream until pale: this will take at least 3–5 minutes, or double that time if beaten by hand. Sift in the flour and rice flour and the flavourings, add a pinch of salt and process very briefly, until just brought together. Do not overprocess.

Tip into a lightly buttered 23 x 33cm/9 x 13in Swiss-roll tin. Using floured hands, press down all over to level the surface. Prick all over with a fork and bake at 150C/300F/ Gas 2 for 40–45 minutes, or until uniformly pale golden brown.

Shake over some sugar from a dredger and cut into squares or fingers. Leave for 5–10 minutes, then carefully remove to a wire rack to cool completely.

7

BRIDE'S BONN

makes 2 rounds (cut into 8 triangles each)

Bride's Bonn is a traditional Shetland cake or bread – formerly it was a sweet oat bannock, then later it became a thick round of shortbread. This was broken over the bride's head by the womenfolk as she entered the house for the wedding party after the church service. The practice was rather like the custom of throwing confetti in our days, though with the shortbread, guests would scrabble for pieces to take home and put under their pillows as they were meant to have special attributes that enhanced dreams: bride's bonn was also traditionally known as Dreaming Bread.

I have introduced self-raising flour to my regular oatmeal shortbread, as it makes it lighter and more short; otherwise the oatmeal, being heavier, makes it too dense.

This is one of my favourite shortbreads – light, nutty and moreish.

200g/7oz butter, softened	200g/7oz self-raising flour, sifted
100g/3½oz golden caster sugar	100g/3½oz medium oatmeal

Cream the butter and sugar together until really creamy and pale: this will take 4–5 minutes in a food mixer or longer by hand.

Now add the combined flour (and pinch of salt) and oatmeal a tablespoonful at a time, only adding more when each is incorporated. When it is all mixed in, bring together with your hands and tip into two prepared tins (lightly buttered 18cm/7in sandwich tins). Using floured hands, press down so the mixture levels out.

Prick all over with a fork (ensure you go right through to the base) and 'scallop' the edges by nicking round the edges with the edge of a spoon or the tines of a fork.

Place in a preheated oven (150C/300F/Gas 2) for 35–40 minutes until golden brown. Remove the tins to a wire rack and cut each into eight triangles. Leave for 15–20 minutes or so, then remove from the tin while still a little warm but firm enough to be moved. Leave on a wire rack until cold.

8

RASPBERRY SHORTBREAD
makes 24 pieces

The idea for this came quite simply because, as I was eating a piece of shortie with the first raspberries of the season and marvelling how well they go together, it occurred to me – why did I not try to combine the two? The result is, to my mind, astonishingly good.

It is essential to use fresh berries, not frozen, and ones that are firm, though ripe. If the berries are soft and squishy, when you tip the shortbread mixture over them they will collapse and ooze pink juices, which is not the point.

This shortbread is a little more fragile than the other shortbreads here, so handle with care. Also, unlike other shortbreads, it does not keep well, so use within a day or freeze till later.

200g/7oz butter, softened

100g/3½oz golden caster sugar + extra to sprinkle

250g/9oz self-raising flour, sifted

70g/2½oz medium oatmeal

200g/7oz fresh raspberries (ripe yet firm)

Cream the butter and sugar together until really creamy and pale: this will take 4–5 minutes in a food mixer and longer by hand.

Now add the combined flour and oatmeal and a pinch of salt, in a couple of batches, only adding more when each batch is incorporated. When it is all mixed in, bring together with your hands.

Meanwhile, butter a Swiss-roll tin (23 x 33cm/9 x 13in).

Arrange the raspberries over the base evenly. Tip the shortbread mixture all over and, using floured hands, gently press down so the mixture levels out. (Don't worry if there are little unfilled patches as, since it's self-raising flour, the mixture will spread out to fill all gaps.) Prick all over with a fork and place in a preheated oven (150C/300F/Gas 2) for 35–40 minutes until golden brown. Remove the tins to a wire rack, sprinkle with a little sugar, then cut each into 24 pieces until completely cold before decanting to wire rack.

CHAPTER SIX

Biscuits

Everyone loves a biscuit. Some might protest they do not, but when offered a little something with their tea, who can refuse? When I used to stay at my Aunt Muriel's home in Dundee, I was given a cup of tea in bed first thing, and with that drink came a biscuit, usually a buttery piece of shortbread or a Royal Scot biscuit. Just what was needed to gear the appetite up for the porridge and Arbroath smokies to follow. And although my own children, when they were young, were always the contrary sort who loved going to friends' houses where they could have such novelties as packet custard creams or foil-wrapped chocolate biscuits, their friends seemed to enjoy the contents of our cookie jars filled with home-made goodies.

The great thing about biscuits is that they keep well and so they can usually last up to a week in a well-sealed jar. They are also eminently versatile, served with morning coffee, afternoon tea, sandwiched together with a scoop of ice-cream for pudding or – for the savoury ones – served with a glass of chilled fino sherry or champagne. And let us not forget that Scots New Year classic, shortbread with a slice of Cheddar and a dram. Perhaps not to be recommended first thing in the morning after a late Hogmanay, however.

Opposite: Oaty Cookie Sandwiches (p.91).

I
OATIES**
makes 12–16 biscuits

These easy biscuits are full of oaty goodness. They are crunchy, light and buttery, ideal to go with morning coffee or an afternoon cup of tea.

For a change, you can add a handful of raisins to make that all-American favourite, oatmeal raisin cookies.

150g/5½oz butter, softened	125g/4½oz porridge oats
50g/1¾oz golden caster sugar	75g/2¾oz self-raising flour, sifted
75g/2¾oz light muscovado sugar	½ tsp bicarbonate of soda

Cream the butter and sugars together until smooth, add the oats, flour, bicarbonate of soda and a pinch of salt. Stir until thoroughly combined, then using floured hands, roll into balls and place – well apart (they will spread) – on greased baking sheets (you will probably need two).

Bake in a preheated oven (180C/350F/Gas 4) for about 15 minutes (swapping over baking sheets if two are in the oven at the same time) or until golden brown. Leave for 2–3 minutes, then remove to a wire rack to continue cooling.

2

GINGER BISCUITS
makes 15–16 biscuits

These are a modern version of F. Marian McNeill's 1929 recipe for 'Snaps'. Her recipe is made with flour, butter, sugar, ground ginger and syrup or treacle. Once they are nearly done she advises brushing with a syrup of sugar and water to give a glaze. I have cut down the amount of sugar and syrup used, as the old recipe must have been inordinately sweet with an astonishing twelve ounces of sugar and four ounces of syrup. They are not as crisp as the old recipe since – thankfully! – they have less sugar.

The snaps are mentioned in Sir Walter Scott's St Ronan's Well, *and called brandy snaps as they were probably flavoured with brandy.*

200g/7oz plain flour, sifted	2 level tsp ground ginger
25g/1oz golden caster sugar	100g/3½oz butter
1 level tsp bicarbonate of soda	2 level tbsp golden syrup

Combine the flour, sugar, bicarbonate of soda and a pinch of salt in a bowl.

In a small saucepan, melt the butter and syrup together and tip into the bowl, stirring to combine. Do not overmix.

Once combined, take off little clumps and roll into balls. Place on two buttered baking sheets, spaced well apart, and using the heel of your hand, press down to flatten slightly.

Bake in a preheated oven (180C/350F/Gas 4) for about 12 minutes, swapping two baking sheets, if used, round halfway. Place on a wire rack and leave to cool completely. (They will firm up on cooling, but are a little soft while hot.)

3
OATY COOKIE SANDWICHES**
makes 12 biscuits/6 sandwiches

Once you have tried these delicious 'sandwiches', they will become a favourite, I can assure you. Two light, crunchy cookies are squished together with the most delicious yet easy lemony cream. Any leftover filling can be popped into a little ramekin, clingfilmed, then frozen and served as rich lemony ice-cream.

100g/3½oz butter, softened	½ tsp baking powder
150g/5½oz light muscovado sugar	*Filling:*
1 medium free-range egg	3 heaped tbsp lemon curd (preferably home-made)
100g/3½oz porridge oats	3 heaped tbsp mascarpone (about 125g/4½oz)
75g/2¾oz plain flour, sifted	

For the biscuits, beat the butter until soft then add the sugar and beat well until light and creamy. (I use my food mixer, but you can easily do it by hand.) Add the egg, beat again and add the oats, flour and baking powder with a pinch of salt. Mix briefly until combined, then using floured hands, roll into 12 balls – each about the size of a ping-pong ball. Place these on buttered baking trays, spaced well apart (use two trays as they will spread a little).

Bake in a preheated oven (180C/350F/Gas 4) for about 12–14 minutes until lightly coloured but not crisp; the centre will be still a little soft.

Remove and leave on their trays for a couple of minutes, then transfer to a wire rack with a metal spatula. Leave to cool.

Beat the curd and mascarpone together for the filling and use a generous spoonful to sandwich two biscuits together.

4
THYME AND CHEESE STRAWS**

makes 12

Ok, these are not exactly classic biscuits, but they are a form of savoury biscuit, everyone's favourite with drinks. Use a good Scottish Cheddar-style cheese such as Mull or Locharthur.

375g sheet of ready-rolled puff pastry

1 medium free-range egg, beaten

75g/2¾oz grated cheese

a couple of sprigs of thyme

sea salt

Lay out the pastry on a large board and brush with the egg. Scatter two thirds of the cheese over one half of the rectangle, leaving a narrow border round the edges. Scatter the thyme leaves over the cheese, season with sea salt and black pepper and fold over the remaining pastry half to enclose. Lightly roll with a rolling pin to seal.

Brush the surface with the egg and scatter over the remaining cheese. Cut into twelve strips, then shape each strip by twisting each end in a different direction. Place these on a baking sheet lined with baking parchment. Bake in a preheated oven (220C/425F/Gas 7) for about 10 minutes until puffed up and golden. Transfer to a wire rack to cool a little, then serve warm. (Or bake in advance and reheat till warm.)

5

PARLIES

makes 16 biscuits

Parlies are a type of gingerbread baked as biscuits. Although soft when you remove them from the oven, they firm up as they cool to become crispy but slightly chewy in the centre. It is important not to overwork the dough or they will be tough.

'Parlies' is short for Parliament Cakes; the name is said to be derived from their popularity with members of the Scots parliament. In late eighteenth-century Edinburgh, a lady called Mrs Flockhart ran a shop and tavern in Potterrow (which is at the back of the Royal Scottish Museum in Chambers Street, in the University area). Although the shop was a general one, the back room was the scene of her most profitable business. Her eminent customers – including Mr Scott (father of Sir Walter) and several Lords – would pass through the front shop to the back room to partake of a dram or two and some gingerbread or biscuits. Her thin, crisp, square cakes were called Parliaments or Parlies, the round ones Snaps and the thick soft cakes White or Brown Quality Cakes.

Paving stones (known as paving stanes) are Fife's equivalent to parlies and are made from a gingerbread-type mixture that is shaped to look like old-fashioned cobbles, which were oblong rather than round. Once baked, a boiled sugar syrup is poured over them to form a crunchy coating.

100g/3½oz butter	50g/1¾oz dark muscovado sugar
2 tbsp black treacle	
200 g/7oz plain flour, sifted	
1 rounded tsp ground ginger	

Melt the butter and treacle together gently.

Mix the flour, ginger, sugar and a pinch of salt in a bowl. Pour in the melted mixture and stir briefly to combine.

Tip into a 23cm/9in square buttered tin and, using floured hands, flatten down. Prick all over.

Bake at 170C/325F/Gas 3 for 18–20 minutes. Remove and cut into squares, then transfer carefully – while warm – to a wire tray to cool.

6

CHEESE AND CARAWAY BISCUITS**

makes 15 biscuits

Caraway adds an unusual flavour to these crispy savoury biscuits. Caraway was used often in centuries past in Scotland, mainly in cakes and shortbread. So, although the spice is a link to the past, the use of parmesan certainly is not!

Serve these with drinks; they are particularly good with champagne.

100g/3½oz plain flour, sifted   100g/3½oz butter, softened

1 tsp caraway seeds

100g/3½oz grated
parmesan cheese

Place the first three ingredients in a food-processor and add the butter in knobs. Whizz until combined, then, with the machine running, add 1 tablespoon of cold water and combine briefly until you can bring the dough together with your hands.

Tip onto a large sheet of clingfilm and roll into a log, about 18cm/7in long. Wrap tightly in the wrap and chill for an hour or so. Then cut into 15 slices and place on a buttered baking sheet. Prick with a fork and bake at 180C/350F/Gas 4 for 18–20 minutes or until golden. Cool on a wire rack.

7
ABERNETHY BISCUITS
makes 12–15 biscuits

Some recipes add a teaspoon of caraway seeds to the basic mixture. F. Marian McNeill suggests a mere half teaspoon for 8oz of flour, which is pretty much the amount used here.

These traditional biscuits are eaten as they are, with a cuppa or sometimes topped with a smear of butter and a slice of cheese. They were an ideal 'shivery bite' (a little snack eaten to warm you up, for example after emerging from freezing cold swimming baths in the olden days!

These are incredibly easy to make, but be careful as the dough is softish, so don't add too much flour when rolling out. A light hand is required!

200 g/7oz plain flour,

1 level tsp baking powder

75g/2¾oz butter, diced

75g/2¾oz golden caster sugar

1 medium free-range egg, beaten

25–50ml/1–2fl oz milk

Sift the flour and baking powder together with a pinch of salt, and rub in the butter until it resembles breadcrumbs. Add the sugar, stir, and mix in the beaten egg with enough milk to form a stiff yet soft dough that you can bring together with your (floured) hands. Turn onto a floured surface and roll out thinly. Cut out into rounds with a 5–6cm/2–2½in cutter.

Place on a buttered baking sheet, prick all over with a fork and bake at 180C/350F/Gas 4 for 12–15 minutes or until pale golden brown. Transfer to a wire rack to cool and firm up.

8

RAGGIE BISCUITS
makes 20 biscuits

Raggie biscuits are a speciality of Fife and were traditionally eaten with a cup of tea, which is why they are also known as Raggie Teas.

Because they are not too sweet, they are also good with cheese. The distinctive prickled appearance of the biscuits is made in bakeries with a special stamp of 'prickles' or tiny holes, but at home, just use the tines of a fork. The holes not only look good, they prevent the biscuits blistering during baking.

250 g/9oz self-raising flour

50g/1¾oz plain flour

75 g/2¾oz golden caster sugar

150 g/5½oz butter, softened

Sift the flours into a food-processor or mixer (or into a mixing bowl) and add the sugar. Add the butter and a pinch of salt and process briefly until it resembles breadcrumbs, then add 75–100ml (2½–3½fl oz) cold water, enough to combine to a dough. (Or do everything by hand: rub in the fat, stir in the water to combine.) Divide the dough into 18–20 small balls. Flatten these slightly and fold in the edges, irregularly. Then turn over and flatten again with a rolling pin. The edges should be nicely ragged – if not, tease some of the dough out to make them look less regular. You want them to be about 5mm/¼in thick. (Any thicker and they will still taste good, but will not be as crispy.)

Place on two greased baking trays, prick all over with a fork and bake at 180C/350F/ Gas 4 for 18–20 minutes until a pale golden brown. Remove to a wire rack. They will crisp up as they are cooling.

CHAPTER SEVEN

Tarts and Pies

I have always loved pies and tarts, sweet and savoury pastries – ever since that classic of my youth, bacon and egg pie, was transformed as if by magic into the 1970s classic, Quiche Lorraine (without much alteration in most cases). I often used to enjoy Scotch pies or Forfar bridies, their perfectly crusty (never hard) outers containing the warm, meaty, gravy-moistened fillings. I have since happily rolled out many a pastry case before filling, then baking and allowing to cool for just long enough, before scoffing with indecent haste. And Border Tart and all its close cousins – Eyemouth and Ecclefechan to name but two – I enjoyed as a child and now still adore both baking and eating. These, just like bridies and Scotch pies, were part of my childhood.

Although puff pastry is handy to buy and there are some excellent all-butter ones available now and good filo pastry is also widely available, I always prefer home-made shortcrust pastry, which can be enhanced by the addition of grated cheese, oatmeal or herbs, and with fillings that can include meat, fish, vegetables or cheese. Savoury pies and tarts are incredibly versatile, suitable for any time of day and for any meal. They freeze well and so you can batch-bake and tuck some in the freezer drawer for another day. If taking a tart or pie to a picnic, bring to the venue in its baking tin and decant from the tin in situ, while the others unfold the tartan travelling rug and uncork the wine.

Opposite: Eyemouth Tart (p.104).

I

DUNDEE APPLE TART

serves 6

This is the apple pie of my childhood, a plate pie, not a deep one. My parents remember pies like this, and they were always called tarts in Dundee, the word pie being reserved for the small Scotch pie or large steak pie. It was usually served with custard and always made on an enamel plate or shallow enamel dish. This is a recipe that reeks of nostalgia.

4 large cooking apples, peeled and thinly sliced

2 heaped tbsp golden caster sugar

1 level tsp cinnamon

juice of 1 lemon

350g/12oz sweet shortcrust pastry (see Paradise Slice recipe on page 62, Traybakes chapter)

milk and sugar to glaze

Place the apples in a microwave bowl with the sugar, cinnamon and lemon juice. Cover tightly and cook for about 5 minutes until softened but still a little firm. Drain over a sieve and cool.

Roll out the pastry to fit a shallow tart tin (approx 23cm/9in), fill with the apples and roll out another piece of pastry to cover. Seal the edges and paint the surface with some milk. Sprinkle with a little sugar.

Slash two holes in the top for the steam to escape, then bake in a preheated oven (190C/375F/Gas 5) for 35–40 minutes or until the pastry is golden.

2

DEEP APPLE PIE WITH BUTTERSCOTCH AND OATY CRUMBLE**

serves 10

This pie is the antithesis of those simple plate apple pies well-loved in Scottish homes. This one is deep and bulging with apples and topped with a crunchy oaty topping. It is hearty and extravagant, a contrast to the humbler yet still delicious plate apple pie of yore!

If you want to make this the day before, I recommend removing the outer ring of the tin when the pie is completely cold, then reheating it on its base in a medium oven until warm.

Pastry:

300g/10½oz plain flour

½ tsp baking powder

40g/1½oz golden caster sugar

200g/7oz butter, cubed

1 medium free-range egg plus 1 medium yolk

Filling:

1 tbsp semolina

1 heaped tbsp plain flour

100g/3½oz light muscovado sugar

2 tsp ground cinnamon

2 kg/4lb 8oz cooking apples

1 x 397g tin of caramel (or dulce de leche)

Crumble topping:

75g/2¾oz plain flour

75g/2¾oz porridge oats

½ tsp ground cinnamon

100g/3½oz butter, slightly softened, cubed

For the pastry, place the first four ingredients in a food-processor and whizz until the mixture resembles breadcrumbs, then, with the motor running, add the egg and yolk.

Once combined, bring the dough together with your hands, clingwrap and chill in the fridge for half an hour or so.

Now roll out and use to line the base and sides of a buttered, deep 23cm/9in. loose-bottom cake tin. Prick the base and chill well, preferably overnight.

Once ready to bake, sprinkle the semolina all over the base.

For the filling, combine the flour, sugar and cinnamon in a large bowl. Peel the apples, chop and add to the bowl, stirring to coat. Tip half into the tin and spoon over about a third of the tin of caramel, dolloping it all over. Add the remaining apples, squashing down with your hands once they are all in. Spoon over the remaining caramel, smoothing over as evenly as you can.

For the crumble, mix together the flour, oats and cinnamon and rub in the butter. Sprinkle this over the caramel-topped apples and press down to ensure an even coating.

Place on a hot baking sheet in the oven preheated to 200C/400F/Gas 6 and bake for 10 minutes, then reduce to 180C/350F/Gas 4 and continue to bake for a further 1 hour 20 minutes (1 hour 30 minutes altogether), covering with foil after the first half hour or so. It is ready when you push a metal skewer carefully through the topping and you can feel the apples are soft.

Allow to stand for an hour or so, then serve warm with custard or ice-cream.

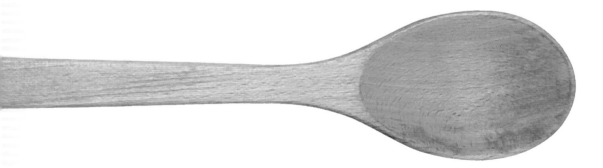

3

BORDER TART

serves 8

This is based on one of my mother's tea-time specials. These days, Border tart is a shortcrust pastry case filled with a rich, spiced raisin filling, to which I add the grated zest of a lemon. Originally it was an enriched yeast pastry case filled with almonds, raisins, peel and marzipan, all bound together in an egg custard. The dough for the base would have been a portion taken from the weekly bread-making.

There are similar tarts to be found all over the Borders, most notably Eyemouth tart, which is similar with raisins and brown sugar in the filling, but the Eyemouth version also adds coconut, walnuts and glacé cherries.

Ecclefechan tart is also similar, without the cherries and coconut; and finally there is Melrose tart, a ginger sponge baked in pastry.

Pastry:	Filling:
150g/5½oz plain flour, sifted	100g/3½oz butter, softened
50g/1¾oz ground almonds	100g/3½oz dark muscovado sugar
125g/4½oz butter, diced	2 large free-range eggs, beaten
25g/1oz golden caster sugar	400g/14oz raisins
1 medium free-range egg, beaten	grated zest of 1 large lemon
	1 level tsp mixed spice

To make the pastry, place the flour, almonds, butter and sugar in a food-processor with a pinch of salt. Process until it resembles breadcrumbs, then add the egg and process briefly, adding a splash of cold water if necessary to bind. Bring the mixture together with your hands, wrap in clingfilm and chill for 1 hour.

Roll out the pastry to fit a shallow 23cm/9in tart tin. Prick the base all over and chill for at least 2 hours, preferably overnight.

Line the pastry case with foil and baking beans and bake at 200C/400F/Gas 6 for 10 minutes, remove the foil and beans and continue to bake for 5 minutes, then take out of the oven. Reduce the temperature to 180C/350F/Gas 4.

For the filling, beat together the butter and sugar and stir in the eggs, raisins, lemon zest and spice. Tip this into the part-baked pastry case and bake in the oven for about 30 minutes until set. You might want to cover the tin loosely with foil for the last 10 minutes or so to prevent the raisins burning. Allow the tart to cool and serve in slices with tea or coffee.

4
EYEMOUTH TART
serves 8

Eyemouth is a fishing town on the south east coast of Scotland, famous for its wonderful seafood – and its tarts!

Pastry:

150g/5½oz plain flour, sifted

75g/2¾oz ground almonds

125g/4½oz butter, diced

25g/1oz golden caster sugar

1 medium free-range egg, beaten

Filling:

100g/3½oz butter, softened

100g/3½oz dark muscovado sugar

2 medium free-range eggs, beaten

250g/9oz raisins

75g/2¾oz desiccated coconut

75g/2¾oz walnuts, chopped

25g/1oz undyed glacé cherries, halved

For the pastry, place the flour, butter and sugar in a food-processor with a pinch of salt. Process until it resembles breadcrumbs and add the egg, with a splash of cold water if necessary to bind. Process briefly, then bring the mixture together with your hands, wrap in clingfilm and chill for 1 hour.

Roll out the pastry to fit a shallow 23cm/9in tart tin. Prick the base all over and chill for at least 2 hours, preferably overnight.

Line the pastry case with foil and baking beans and bake at 200C/400F/Gas 6 for 10 minutes, remove the foil and beans and continue to bake for 5 minutes, then take out of the oven. Reduce the temperature to 180C/350F/Gas 4.

For the filling, beat together the butter and sugar and stir in the remaining ingredients. Tip into the pastry case and bake in the oven for about 30 minutes or until set, covering loosely with foil for the last 10 minutes to prevent the raisins burning.

5

ECCLEFECHAN TART

serves 8

A variation of the classic Border tart, this is from Ecclefechan – a town in the south-west of the Borders – but has the addition of walnuts and cinnamon. You can substitute pecans for the walnuts and indeed, to my mind, an Ecclefechan tart is leagues better than America's pecan pie.

Serve this cold for tea – or barely warm with a dollop of whipped cream and perhaps a scattering of chopped toasted walnuts on top.

Pastry:

200g/7oz plain flour, sifted

115g/4oz butter, diced

25g/1oz golden caster sugar

1 large free-range egg, beaten

Filling:

115g/4oz butter, softened

115g/4oz dark muscovado sugar

2 large free-range eggs, beaten

300g/10½oz raisins

grated zest of 1 large unwaxed lemon + 1 tbsp lemon juice

100g/3½oz walnuts, chopped

½ tsp ground cinnamon

For the pastry, place the flour, butter and sugar in a food-processor with a pinch of salt. Process until it resembles breadcrumbs, add the egg, process briefly again and bring the mixture together with your hands, wrap in clingfilm and chill for 1 hour.

Roll out the pastry to fit a shallow 23cm/9in tart tin. Prick the base all over and chill for at least 2 hours, preferably overnight.

Line the pastry case with foil and baking beans and bake at 200C/400F/Gas 6 for 10 minutes, remove the foil and beans and continue to bake for 5 minutes, then remove from the oven. Reduce the temperature to 180C/350F/Gas 4.

For the filling, beat together the butter and sugar and stir in the eggs, raisins, lemon zest, juice, nuts and spices. Tip into the pastry case and bake in the oven for about 30 minutes or until set, covering loosely with foil for the last 10 minutes to prevent the raisins burning.

Allow the tart to cool and serve cold for afternoon tea – or warm for pudding, with cream and toasted nuts.

6

TREACLE TART**

serves 8

In Scotland, we have never really understood treacle tart. Don't get me wrong, it's not that we don't like it – heavily sweet with syrup and stodgy with breadcrumbs and perhaps a nod to health with a squeeze of jiffy lemon. But we just wonder why it's not called syrup tart. For in Scotland golden syrup is syrup and black treacle is treacle; in England treacle means both syrup and black treacle, presumably because black treacle is used less.

So, in this tasty teatime tart, I have added some black treacle and zapped up the fresh lemon flavour so it is zingy rather than cloying. I think this might be appreciated north and south of the border.

Pastry:	1 tbsp black treacle
175g/6oz plain flour, sifted	zest and juice of 1 lemon
25g/1oz golden caster sugar	25g/1oz butter
100g/3½oz butter, diced	150g/5½oz fresh white breadcrumbs
1 medium free-range egg	
Filling:	2 medium free-range eggs, beaten
450g tin of golden syrup	

For the pastry, place the flour, sugar and butter in a food-processor and whizz until it resembles breadcrumbs. Slowly add the egg through the feeder tube, stop the machine and bring together with your hands to a ball. Clingwrap and chill for at least an hour, then roll out to fit a shallow 23cm/9in tart tin. Prick all over the base and chill well, preferably overnight.

For the filling, heat the syrup, treacle, lemon juice and zest and butter till melted, simmering for a couple of minutes before removing from the heat and stirring in the breadcrumbs. Set aside for about 20 minutes and then stir in the eggs.

Fill the baking case with foil and baking beans and bake at 200C/400F/Gas 6 for 15 minutes; remove the foil and beans and continue to bake for 5 minutes or so until just cooked. Remove and cool a little, then fill with the breadcrumb mixture. Bake at 170C/325F/Gas 3 for about 30 minutes until almost set. (There should still be a little wobble in the centre.) Remove and allow to become barely warm before cutting.

7

RHUBARB TART

serves 8

Just like apple tart, this is another 'plate' pie well-loved throughout Scotland. In Dundee it is always called a tart, even though the distinction elsewhere between tart and pie is often that a tart has no pastry lid. But for my parents it was always apple or rhubarb tart baked on a shallow enamel plate. Unless of course you went to a bakers (no one made these at home)

and bought some dinky little rhubarb pies – shaped like a Scotch pie but sweet and oozing with pink syrupy juices.

Though not traditional, you can add some finely chopped stem ginger (1–2 balls) from a jar of ginger in syrup.

Pastry:

250g/9oz self-raising flour, sifted

150g/5½oz butter, cubed

50g/1¾oz icing sugar, sifted

1 medium free-range egg

Filling:

400g/14oz rhubarb (preferably young and pink), trimmed and chopped

2 tbsp plain flour

90g/3¼oz light muscovado sugar

chopped stem ginger, optional

Glaze:

1 free-range egg yolk

golden caster sugar

For the pastry, combine the flour, butter and sugar in a food-processor, then, with the machine running, add the egg and whizz until the mixture is a little clumpy. Combine with your hands and wrap in clingfilm. Chill for an hour or so, then roll out half to fit a buttered 23cm/9in enamel pie plate.

For the filling, combine everything together and tip into the pie.

Roll out the remaining pastry, dampen the edges and use to cover the fruit. Trim the edges of the pastry.

Glaze by brushing all over with the egg yolk, sprinkling with sugar. Using scissors, snip a little hole. Chill for 10–15 minutes until the egg sets, then bake in a preheated oven (200C/400C/Gas 6) for 30–35 minutes, covering loosely with foil after the first 15 minutes to prevent the pastry burning. Test it is ready by poking through the hole with a metal skewer to check that the rhubarb is tender. Serve warm, not hot, with thick cream or custard.

8

FORFAR BRIDIE
makes 4

*Bridies and pies are still very much a part of life in Dundee and Angus.
And whereas the best pies have traditionally come from Dundee, the best
bridies are from Forfar. J.M. Barrie mentioned bridies in one of the novels
he wrote at the end of the nineteenth and early twentieth centuries. He
was native of Kirriemuir, some five miles north-west of Forfar and so
would have been very familiar with the bridies of Angus. According to F.
Marian McNeill, the first Forfar bridie baker was a Mr Jolly in the mid-
nineteenth century.*

*My recipe is based on Bill McLaren's, whose great-grandfather, James
McLaren, learned the skills of bridie-making at Jolly's bakery. His family-
run bakery, which opened in 1893, has baked bridies to the same recipe
ever since. When I visited him, he taught me about the essential 'dunting'
and 'nicking' procedure to seal the horseshoe-shaped bridie. The 'dunting'
is done with the heel of the hand, pressing down on the edges. The 'nicking'
is done with forefinger and thumb, to finish the sealing.*

Reheat the bridies to eat warm.

Pastry:	Filling:
250g/9oz strong white flour	450g/1lb shoulder or rump beef
50g/1¾oz plain flour	
75g/2¾oz butter, cubed	75g/2¾oz beef suet, grated
50g/1¾oz dripping (or white fat), cubed	1 small onion, peeled and finely grated

For the pastry, sift the flours and a pinch of salt into a food-processor. Add the butter
and dripping fats and process until incorporated. Add just enough cold water (2–3 tbsp)
to bind to a stiff dough. Gather in your hands, wrap in clingfilm and chill for at least 1
hour.

For the filling, roughly chop the beef – I use the pulse button on my food-processor. Alternatively, mince very coarsely. Mix together the beef, suet, onion and plenty of salt and pepper. The mixture should be fairly stiff.

Divide the pastry into four and roll each piece into an oval, the widest diameter of which is about 23cm/9in. Divide the filling into four and spoon onto one half of each pastry oval, leaving a border all round.

Dampen the edges and fold the top half of the pastry over the filling to enclose it. Trim the edges into a neat horseshoe shape (not a half-moon: that is the Cornish pasty). Now dunt and nick – by pressing down the edges to seal and crimping all around to give a nicely finished look. Using a sharp knife, prick a small hole (for steam to escape) in the top of each bridie. Place on a lightly buttered baking tray and chill for an hour or so.

Bake in a preheated oven (200C/400F/Gas 6) for 30–35 minutes or until golden brown. Serve warm.

9
CULLEN SKINK BRIDIES**
makes 4

These wonderful bridies, based on the flavours of Scotland's Cullen Skink soup, are ideal for non-meat eaters – they are made from smoked haddock and flavoured with mustard and lemon. Delicious!

Pastry:

250g/9oz strong white flour

75g/2¾oz plain flour

175g/6oz butter, cubed

Filling:

500g/1lb 2oz undyed
smoked haddock fillets

300ml/10fl oz whole milk

3 tbsp freshly chopped flat
parsley plus parsley stalks

25g/1oz butter

25g/1oz plain flour

2 heaped tsp Dijon mustard

grated zest of 1 lemon

For the pastry, sift the flours and a pinch of salt into a food-processor. Add the butter and process until incorporated. Add just enough cold water (2–3 tbsp) to bind to a stiff dough. Gather in your hands, wrap in clingfilm and chill for at least 1 hour.

For the filling, place the fish in a saucepan with the milk and parsley stalks. Bring slowly to the boil, bubble for 1 minute, remove from the heat and cover. Leave for half an hour or so, then strain through a sieve into a jug. Melt the butter in a saucepan, add the flour and stir for a minute. Now add the reserved fish liquor and, whisking, cook over a medium-low heat until smooth. Stir in the mustard, lemon zest, chopped parsley leaves and seasoning to taste. Cool.

Divide the pastry into four and roll each piece into an oval, the widest diameter of which is about 23cm/9in. Divide the filling into four and spoon onto one half of each pastry oval, leaving a border all round.

Dampen the edges and fold the top half of the pastry over the filling to enclose it. Trim the edges into a neat horseshoe shape. Now dunt and nick – by pressing down the edges to seal and crimping all around to give a nicely finished look. Using a sharp knife, prick a small hole (for steam to escape) in the top of each bridie.

Place on a lightly buttered baking tray and chill for an hour or so.

Bake in a preheated oven (200C/400F/Gas 6) for about 40 minutes, or until a pale golden brown. Serve warm.

10

VENISON BRIDIES
makes 4

Venison was used often in the past in Scotland instead of both beef and lamb, as deer roamed the country before the widespread influx of sheep during and after the Highland Clearances of the eighteenth and nineteenth centuries.

The venison bridie is delicious and mouth-watering. Enjoy with a glass of red and a salad, both of which are of course rather un-Forfar.

Pastry:

250g/9oz strong white flour

75g/2¾oz plain flour

175g/6oz butter, cubed

Filling:

500g/1lb 2oz venison mince
(usually taken from the shin),
coarsely, not finely minced

75g/2¾oz beef suet, grated

1 small onion, peeled and
finely grated

1 heaped tbsp fresh parsley,
finely chopped

For the pastry, sift the flours and half tsp salt into a food-processor. Add the fats and process until incorporated. Add just enough cold water (about 3 tbsp) to bind to a stiff dough. Gather in your hands, wrap in clingfilm and chill for at least 1 hour.

For the filling, mix the venison, suet, onion, parsley and plenty of salt and pepper.

Divide the pastry into four and roll each piece into an oval. Divide the filling into four and spoon onto one half of each pastry oval, leaving a border all round.

Dampen the edges and fold the top half of the pastry over the filling to enclose it. Trim the edges into a neat horseshoe shape. Now 'dunt' and 'nick', by pressing down the edges to seal and crimping all around to give a nicely finished look. Using a sharp knife, prick a small hole (for steam to escape) in the top of each bridie. Place on a lightly buttered baking tray and chill for an hour or so.

Bake in a preheated oven (200C/400F/Gas 6) for 35–40 minutes or until golden brown. Serve warm, not hot.

11

PARTAN BREE TART

serves 8

Partan bree is one of Scotland's traditional soups — a rich, creamy crab soup. Partan means crab, bree means liquid or gravy. Typical in many seaside areas of Scotland, this recipe has of course many variations. Lady

Clark of Tillypronie in her 1909 book suggests adding some anchovy, and so I like to finish the tart with a few of these on top.

Don't overdo the mace flavouring – a quarter-teaspoon seems a small amount but it's just enough to give that wonderful background hint without being overpowering.

If you use a large live crab as your base for this recipe, simply boil it for 15–20 minutes, then remove the creamy brown (body) meat to one bowl and the sweet white (claw and leg) meat to another. Discard the feathery 'dead men's fingers' as you work. Otherwise, fresh or defrosted frozen crab will do.

This amount of pastry will give you some left over – enough to roll out thinly, and cut into 5–6 little savoury biscuits. Prick these, then bake at 180C/350F/Gas 4 for about 15 minutes until pale golden.

Pastry:	Filling:
200g/7oz plain flour, sifted	400g/14oz crabmeat (white and brown)
50g/1¾oz freshly grated parmesan	
	4 medium free-range eggs
150g/5½oz butter, diced	¼ tsp ground mace
1 large free-range egg, beaten	300ml tub of crème fraiche
	50g tin of anchovies, drained

For the pastry, place the first three ingredients in a food-processor with a pinch of salt. Process briefly then, with the machine running, add the egg. Bring together with your hands, clingwrap and chill for half an hour or so.

Roll out to fit a 28cm/11in tart tin, prick all over and chill well – preferably overnight. Fill with foil and baking beans and bake blind at 190C/375F/Gas 5 for 15 minutes, remove the foil and cook for a further 5 minutes. Remove and cool.

Beat together the first four filling ingredients with plenty of salt and pepper (taste it if you can bear to, to ensure you have just enough seasoning, adding more salt and pepper if necessary) and pour into the pastry case. Top with the anchovies, arranged like spokes in a wheel, and bake for 40–45 minutes until set and tinged with golden brown. Serve warm or cold, not hot.

12

CINNAMON NABLAB

makes about 20 squares

At the But 'n' Ben, Auchmithie, near Arbroath, is to be found some of the finest traditional home-cooking. Margaret Horn's son Angus is now in charge in the kitchen where Margaret was head chef for many years. In the kitchen, the best of local produce, such as the marvellous fresh shellfish and fish, especially Arbroath Smokies, is used: everything is home-made – from the jam to spread on the towering scones, to the soups, puddings and cakes.

One of my favourites from the magnificent cake trolley is Cinnamon Nablab – a pastry base with a currant filling, spiced sponge topping, and cinnamon-flavoured icing. This is a speciality which Margaret, who was born and bred in the tiny hamlet of Auchmithie, remembers from her childhood. Nablabs have been around for many years in Arbroath. To supplement the nablabs the Auchmithie villagers made themselves at home, there were regular deliveries in baker's vans from nearby Arbroath.

In the baker's shops in Arbroath, there have traditionally been three types of nablab: one topped with brown (cinnamon) icing, another with white icing, and a very special pink-iced nablab which used to have sixpences wrapped up in the cake mix. Although both white and brown iced nablabs have a currant filling, the pink-iced one usually has a jam filling, making it reminiscent of a bakewell pudding or tart.

The etymology of nablab is interesting: in north-eastern Scots dialect, nab – sometimes written 'knab' – means a morsel of food, or a bite. Lab ('leb' or 'laib') means to lick or gobble up. Perhaps nablabs were – after the famous Smokie – Arbroath's first 'fast food'!

Although Margaret has always made her Cinnamon Nablab in a round 25cm/10in deep tin, my adaptation of her recipe here fits a Swiss-roll tin.

Pastry:

350g/12oz sweet shortcrust pastry (use the recipe from Paradise Slice on page 62 (Traybakes chapter)

Filling:

200g/7oz currants

4 tbsp water

75g/2¾oz light muscovado sugar

1 heaped tsp ground cinnamon

2 level tbsp cornflour, slaked in 2 tbsp water

Cake:

225g/8oz butter, softened

225g/8oz golden caster sugar

4 free-range medium eggs

225g/8oz self-raising flour, sifted

1 tsp ground cinnamon

Icing:

200g/7oz icing sugar, sifted

2 heaped tsp ground cinnamon

about 2 tbsp water

First roll out the pastry. Roll out to fit a lightly greased Swiss-roll tin (23cm x 33cm/9in x 13in). Prick all over with a fork. If time permits, leave in the fridge overnight. (If not, leave for at least two hours.)

For the filling, place the currants and water in a small saucepan. Bring slowly to the boil, then stir in the sugar and cinnamon. Reduce the heat slightly and add the slaked cornflour, then, stirring constantly, bring to the boil and cook for a couple of minutes until thickened. Allow to cool for a least 10 minutes.

For the cake, place the butter in a food mixer. Beat well until really soft, add the sugar and beat well – vigorously – until creamy and light. Add the eggs, one at a time, beating well after each addition, adding a spoonful of flour after the second egg. Then fold in the remaining flour and cinnamon.

Spread the fruit filling over the pastry base and top with the cake mix, spreading it well out to cover the filling completely. Place in a preheated oven (200C/400F/ Gas 6) for about 30–35 minutes, until it is well risen and a wooden cocktail stick, inserted in the middle, comes out clean. Cover with foil for the last 10 minutes or so to prevent burning. Leave to cool completely.

Then cut into four large sections and carefully decant these (with a fish slice) onto a wire rack. Beat all the icing ingredients together and spread over the cooled cake. Leave the icing to set, then cut into sections – depending on greed – about 20 altogether.

CHAPTER EIGHT

Oatcakes, Pancakes and Bannocks

Oatcakes have been part of the Scots' staple diet for centuries, with references to Scottish soldiers packing in their bags some oatmeal and a broad metal plate on which to cook oatcakes. It is recorded that Bonnie Prince Charlie's patriotic Highland soldiers set up roadside stalls to provide fresh oatmeal bannocks. The word bannock is interchangeable with oatcake in the west of Scotland. In the east and north-east, a bannock usually contains a proportion of wheat flour with the oatmeal to make a softer version. In this chapter, an oatcake means a crisp little biscuit.

Baked traditionally on the girdle, they can also be baked in the oven, which means you don't have to keep constantly checking that they are not burning. Eaten traditionally for breakfast, they were also used to make sandwiches ('pieces') instead of bread. I can highly recommend them buttered, topped with mature cheese (farmhouse cheddar or goats cheese) and sandwiched with another oatcake on top. This is crumbly and messy – but memorable – picnic food. And to my mind it beats the sandwich of fish-liver between oatcakes that fishermen took to sea with them in the days before sandwich-spread and focaccia.

Opposite: Seeded Oatcakes (p.123).

I
OATCAKES
makes 8 oatcakes

Although oatcakes are traditionally made on the girdle, I have given an oven method below, since most cooks are more familiar with baking trays than girdles. The girdle method is also given; the classic way is to cook on one side on the girdle, then to toast them on a special toasting stone in front of the fire. A brief spell in a low oven will also finish them off. The reason they are not turned over on the girdle to finish the cooking is that this would make them tough.

Once cool, oatcakes are traditionally stored in a 'girnel' (oatmeal chest) to keep crisp. I bury mine in a large tupperware box I keep porridge oats in. The finished texture will depend on the type of oatmeal you use: I like to use a base of medium and either pinhead or fine, for a smooth – or rough – texture. There are also regional variations on the thickness of the oatcake, from thin and crispy to thick and rough.

In the following recipe, depending on how rough or fine you want the texture to be, you can use all oatmeal (200g/7oz) and leave out the pinhead and porridge oats, but I find the combination does give give a good coarse bite without being too crunchy.

150g/5½oz medium oatmeal	½ tsp salt
25g/1oz pinhead oatmeal	½ tsp baking powder
25g/1oz porridge oats	50g/1¾oz butter

Place the first five ingredients in bowl and stir. Melt the butter in 50ml/2fl oz boiling water, combine this with the oats and mix briefly to form a fairly stiff dough.

Sprinkle some oatmeal (fine or medium) over a board and gently roll out the mixture thinly to a circle, about 23cm/9in diameter. Cut into eight wedges and transfer these carefully to a buttered oven tray. Bake at 170C/325F/Gas 3 for about 20 minutes until just firm. Transfer carefully to a wire rack to cool.

Girdle method

Bake the oatcakes, four at a time, on a lightly buttered girdle over a moderate heat for 4–5 minutes on one side only. Once they are light brown underneath, transfer to a wire rack. Place this on a baking tray and set in a low oven (140C/275F/Gas 1) for about 25 minutes or until they have completely dried out.

2
SEEDED OATCAKES**
makes 24–28 oatcakes

These are a doddle to make and are very versatile. They are also less fragile than the traditional ones made from only oats, without the flour I add here. Instead of the seeds listed below, you can add golden linseed or sesame seeds; or add a tablespoon of freshly chopped thyme leaves instead. Serve smeared with butter and with a slice of cheese.

175g/6oz medium oatmeal + extra	1 tbsp poppy seeds
100g/3½oz wholemeal self-raising flour	1 tbsp tsp sunflower seeds
	75g/2¾oz butter

Mix the oatmeal and flour and add the seeds, a grinding of black pepper and a half teaspoon salt. Melt the butter with 150ml/5fl oz hot water and pour this into the bowl, stirring gently with a metal spoon until combined; you might not need all the liquid.

Sprinkle a large board generously with oatmeal and tip out the mixture, combing into a ball with hands dabbed in oatmeal. Roll out thinly, then cut out into rounds, using a fluted cutter.

Place on a greased baking sheet and bake at 150C/300F/Gas 2 for about 45 minutes or until cooked through and crisp. Cool on a wire rack.

3

SCOTCH PANCAKES
makes 12–16 pancakes

'Scotch' pancake to Sassenachs, simply 'pancakes' to Scots. They are also known as 'drop scones' down south, because the batter is loose enough to be dropped onto the girdle.

This is fast food as it was meant to be. From mixing the ingredients for these pancakes to eating them warm, with a cup of tea, takes as little as 10 minutes. And what could be more delicious or easy than making pancakes to eat with butter and jam – either on a girdle or in a frying pan.

This is based on my mother's recipe, though Mum always used plain flour with cream of tartar and bicarbonate of soda instead of self-raising flour. If you have never used a girdle before, it is easy: you can test it is hot enough by dropping a teaspoonful of the batter onto the surface. It should set almost at once – and, if it begins to bubble after 1 minute, the girdle is ready. It is the large bubbles that tell you the pancakes are ready to be flipped over.

Since they are best eaten immediately after being made, you can make a batch and freeze for some later date.

150g/5½oz self-raising flour, sifted	1 large free-range egg, beaten
¼ tsp bicarbonate of soda	175ml/6fl oz milk
1 level tbsp golden caster sugar	

Sift the first two ingredients into a bowl and add a pinch of salt. Stir in the sugar and make a well in the middle.

Add the egg and, with a balloon whisk, whisk together and gradually add the milk, whisking all the time. Continue whisking until you have a smooth batter.

Preheat the girdle (or large heavy frying pan) to medium. Using a piece of kitchen paper, smear it all over with a thin film of butter. Once it is hot (mine takes 4–5 minutes to heat up over a low heat) drop spoonfuls of batter onto the girdle, four at a time. If you want dainty little ones, use a dessertspoon; for slightly larger, use a tablespoon. After about 1½–2 minutes you will notice large bubbles forming on the surface of each. Using a spatula, flip each one over and continue cooking for a further 1–1½ minutes until just done. (They should take about 3–3½ minutes altogether.) Continue with the remaining batter, re-smearing the girdle with a tiny amount of butter for each batch.

Remove and keep warm – I put them in a folded tea towel over a wire rack – then serve with butter and jam.

4

BEREMEAL BANNOCKS
makes 2 bannocks

This is my adaptation of Paul Doull's recipe from Foveran Hotel near Kirkwall on Orkney. Bere is the ancient barley that has grown on the islands for many centuries, and it is still milled in an old watermill and ground into beremeal.

These Orcadian specialities are delicious served with butter and soused herring, smoked salmon paté or a farmhouse cheese.

75g/2¾oz beremeal

75g/2¾oz self-raising flour

1 level tsp bicarbonate of soda

1 rounded tsp cream of tartar

100ml/3½fl oz buttermilk

First put the girdle or solid frying pan on to heat to a steady heat: this can take at least 5 minutes. Very lightly butter the surface.

Mix the flours, soda, cream of tartar and ¼ tsp salt in a bowl. Make a well in the middle and add the buttermilk, then enough cold water to combine to a soft dough (75–100ml/2½–3½fl oz). Tip onto a board dusted with a little beremeal and shape gently into two bannock shapes: rounds about 12cm/4½in diameter and about 2.5cm/1in thick (they puff up as they cook). Use a very light touch and do not knead.

Slap them onto the girdle and cook, without touching, for 5 minutes, then turn and continue to cook for 4 minutes. Both top and bottom will be scorched all over to a golden brown. Remove and place on a wire rack, loosely covered with a tea towel to keep the top soft. Tempting though it is to devour them hot, leave until cold before splitting open and spreading with a little butter.

5

CHEESY OATCAKES
makes 18–20 oatcakes

These crispy oatcakes are good served with a smear of butter or soft goats' cheese. They are also wonderful with a sliver of blue cheese and a spoonful of crunchy honeycomb.

25g/1oz porridge oats

125g/4½oz medium oatmeal

50g/1¾oz self-raising flour

50g/1¾oz finely grated mature Cheddar cheese

25g/1oz butter

Place the oats, oatmeal, flour, cheese and ½ tsp salt in a bowl. Melt the butter in 100ml/3½ml hot water until it is all liquid. Then slowly add this to the mixture in the bowl and combine into a ball with your hands. Do not overwork.

Roll out gently on a lightly floured board and cut into rounds with a biscuit cutter. Transfer to a buttered baking tray and bake in a preheated oven (170C/325F/Gas 3) for about 30 minutes or until they have crisped up and are cooked through. Transfer to a wire rack to cool.

6

PORRIDGE OATCAKES

makes 8–10 oatcakes

So-called as they are made from porridge oats only – no flour is involved, so they are good for anyone with a wheat allergy. They are also rolled in oatmeal instead of flour. They are a doddle to make but are a little fragile, so handle with care when removing from the baking tray.

200g/7oz porridge oats

¼ tsp salt

¼ tsp bicarbonate of soda

25g/1oz butter or lard, melted

Mix the oats, salt and bicarbonate of soda in a bowl.

Melt the butter and add to the bowl, with enough hot water (about 75ml/2½fl oz) to combine to a stiff paste. On a board dusted with oatmeal, pat or roll out thinly as possible and cut into 8–10 rounds. Place on a buttered baking sheet and bake at 170C/325F/Gas 3 for 35–40 minutes. Remove to a wire rack to cool.

7

FATTY CUTTIES

makes 8

This recipe comes from the Orkneys and on each of the many islands there, there are variations. Some have more butter, some more dried fruit, some still have a little beremeal as well as plain flour.

The Orcadian fatty cuttie originated many years ago when people were very poor and daily bread took the form of a girdle bannock, usually made from beremeal. As people became slightly better off they began to use plain wheat flour instead of barley and also began to add fat (butter) to their griddle breads and cakes. Eventually these fat-enriched cakes came to be known as fatty cuttie because they contained some fat and because they were cut into wedges or quarters before baking. A similar dish is the Shetland 'fatty brunnies', which are thick cakes (of oatmeal and/or wheatflour) baked on the girdle and enriched with a lump of lard, to keep them soft.

The fatty cuttie is not dissimilar to Northumberland's Singin' Hinnie and also Wales' famous Welsh cakes, both of which are also baked on the girdle.

175g/6oz plain flour	75g/2¾oz butter, melted
¼ tsp bicarbonate of soda	approx. 1 tbsp milk
75g/2¾oz golden caster sugar	butter, to grease
75g/2¾oz currants	

Sift the flour and bicarbonate of soda into a mixing bowl. Stir in the sugar and currants and pour in the melted butter with just enough milk to combine to a stiff dough. You may need to add another ½–1 tbsp. Knead very lightly and divide into two balls.

Roll each ball into a round shape, about 5mm/¼ inch thick, and cut into four wedges. Pre-heat your girdle or heavy frying pan to medium-hot, grease very lightly and cook the fatty cutties for 3–4 minutes on each side, until golden brown. Serve warm without butter or cold with a thin smear of butter. Always eat on the day they are made.

8

SAUTY BANNOCKS

makes 12 bannocks

These are called sauty bannocks from the French verb 'sauter', to throw or toss; a relic of the Auld Alliance as a result of which, before the Union of the Crowns in 1603, many French words were used in Scottish kitchens. My recipe is based on one from Elizabeth Cleland's New and Easy Method of Cookery written in 1755, which still used – as we do now – culinary terms derived from the French. We still call a leg of lamb a gigot and a large platter an ashet ('assiette').

According to F. Marian McNeill, sauty bannocks were made on Shrove Tuesday and were traditionally made from oatmeal, eggs, beef 'bree' (broth) or milk and cooked on a hot girdle rubbed with fat. She writes, 'The making of the bannocks was a great ploy, in which all present participated.'

The original recipe for these delicious oatmeal pancakes called for 'a chopin of milk' to be boiled and a 'mutchkin of oatmeal' to be stirred in first. The flavourings below (lemon, nutmeg) are what Mrs Cleland stipulated. And her serving suggestion was: 'serve hot with beat [sic] butter, orange, and sugar'.

They are light yet with a good, nutty texture from the oatmeal. An ideal breakfast pancake.

300ml/10fl oz milk	25g/1oz golden caster sugar
125g/4½oz medium oatmeal	tiny grating of nutmeg
	grated zest of 1 lemon
2 medium free-range eggs, beaten	½ tsp baking powder

Bring the milk to the boil and gradually stir in the oatmeal, a little at a time. Once it is all added, remove from the heat. Now, get in with a balloon whisk and beat madly to ensure no lumps. Allow to cool, then beat in the remaining ingredients and a pinch of salt.

Heat a girdle (or heavy frying pan) to medium-hot and lightly wipe with butter. Once hot, drop dessertspoonfuls onto the surface and cook as for Scotch pancakes: 2–3 minutes on one side then, once large bubbles appear, flip over and continue to cook the other side. After 1–2 minutes, remove and keep warm by covering with a teacloth.

Next page: Cheesy Oatcakes (p.126).

Further Reading

Lady Clark of Tillypronie, *The Cookery Book of Lady Clark of Tillypronie*, 1909

Mistress Margaret Dods, *The Cook and Housewife's Manual*, 1829

Theodora Fitzgibbon, *A Taste of Scotland*, 1970

Marion Lochhead, *The Scots Household in the Eighteenth Century*, 1948

F. Marian McNeill, *The Scots Kitchen*, 1929, new edition 2010

INDEX

SUE LAWRENCE

is a food writer and journalist who has written many books on cooking and baking, including *Scottish Kitchen* (2002), *The Sue Lawrence Book of Baking* (2004), *A Cook's Tour of Scotland* (2006) and *Eating In* (2011). Born in Dundee, she was brought up and educated in Edinburgh, later working as a journalist with D.C. Thomson. She was the winner of *MasterChef* (BBC TV) in 1991. President of the Guild of Food Writers from 2004 to 2008, she has received many awards, including a Glenfiddich Award in 2003. She lives in Edinburgh.

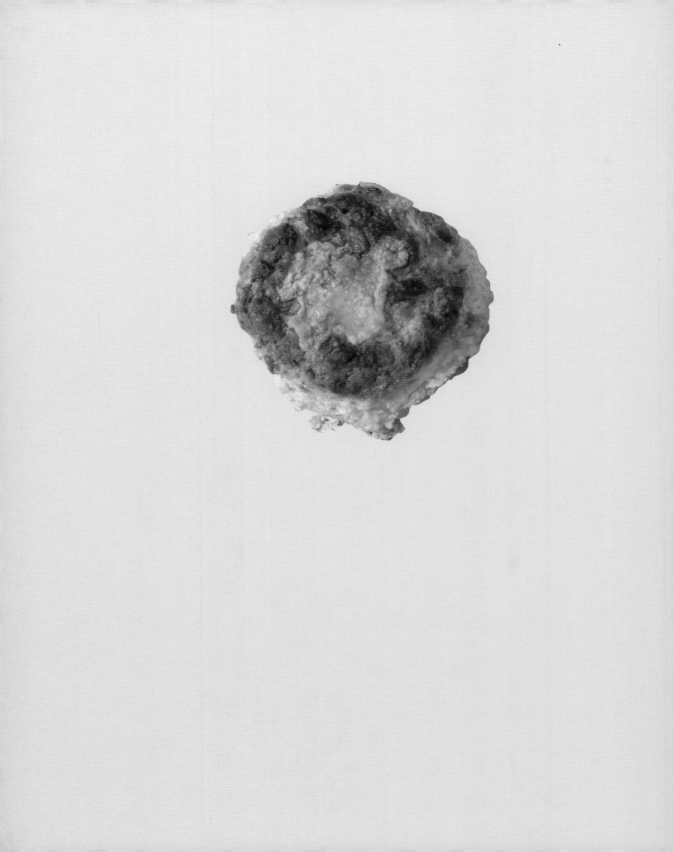